The Revelations

To Pastor Car
with thanks.
May God continue to.
bless you in your ministry

(handwritten inscription)

Mission Control

(A collection of sermons)

Volume Two

Written by

Linda Green

The Revelations of Jesus
Volume One

Front cover image by Paul Thompson FreeBibleimages

ISBN:9781915327307
Book Cover Design: Listening To Your Voice Publishing
Editor: Linda Green
Typesetter: Ruth Pearson
Proof-reader: Cara Green

TABLE OF CONTENTS

Dedication

This book is dedicated to my husband Robert, who has been a constant rock of support, and encouragement as I have researched, written and delivered sermons for years, and to my children and grandchildren, who always support me. I love you all with all my heart.

I would also like to dedicate this book to my mother, who is a prayer warrior supporting me with her prayers, and my siblings whom I love deeply.

To those who read this book, I wish that you find the joy that I found as I studied the book of Revelation. May your walk with Jesus grow deeper and stronger through the blessings found in this unique book.

May God bless you all!

Acknowledgements

I must first acknowledge my God and Saviour, who has shown His wonderful love for humanity and for me. The Creator, who is intimately involved in our salvation, all thanks and praise go to Him. Creator of heaven and earth, the One who loves us with an everlasting love, and has done and will do all He can to save us. This book would not exist without the inspiration and leading of my Lord and Saviour, Jesus Christ, who has guided me, taught me, and moved me throughout this process.

I would also like to thank Pastor Austin, Senior Pastor of the Bread of Life Church, for reading the manuscript and encouraging me in this endeavour.

I must acknowledge Pasto Carl Palmer of the Baptist Church and trainer of the 'Walk Through the Bible' programme. A programme that is well worth doing and supporting as it introduces people to the geography and stories of the Bible in an interactive and fun way. I do not have sufficient words to thank you for your feedback and your prayers.

A big thank you must go to Pastor Humphrey Walters of the Seventh-day Adventist Church, for taking time out of his very busy schedule to read this book and for his feedback and guidance, which has been invaluable and helpful. Thank you for your kind words of encouragement.

Annette Pearson, of Listening To Your Voice Publishing, the thought of publishing a book had not entered my mind. Thank you for being the instrument through which God confirmed to me that I needed to write this book. Annette has been a massive source of support.

I would also like to acknowledge The London Seventh-day Adventist Churches for being the patient recipients of my sermons over the years.

Thank you to Yahushua for the picture of the Tabernacle of Moses

For the picture of the cherubim, I would also like to acknowledge and thank:
Ezekiel Illustration provided by:
John8thirtytwo Publishing
Victoria, B.C., Canada
www.John8thirtytwo.com

A very big thank you to TheBibleSays.com, who I must acknowledge for their generosity in sharing 'Inside the tabernacle' on line, giving readers freedom to share.

I would like to thank 'Dwelling in the Word' for their article on Ezekiel 1 which included the Four faced creature used in this book.

Thank you to McKenzie Jones of McKenzie Blaze for the 'Wheel within a wheel' and 'God on the throne' pictures used with permission in this book.

I want to acknowledge Photo by Harli Marten on Unsplash, Internet cited on 05.03.2023, at:
https://unsplash.com/photos/n7a2OJDSZns

A big thank you to 'Thattheworldmayknow' for the ark of the covenant picture.

'Eyeofprophecy' thank you for the Ark of the covenant with shekinah glory picture.

A massive thank you to Paul Allen for the picture of 'The Lamb with Seven Horns and Seven Eye', Fine Art America.

I also want to acknowledge all the wonderful people who made their pictures available to the public via Wikipedia Commons. I pray blessings on you for your generosity. Thank you to:

- Robert M. Lavinsky for his picture of a ruby and also of Topaz
- Stanislav Doronenko for his picture of a jasper stone
- Geni for their picture of an emerald
- Ariely for the picture of the Menorah
- Wardyboy400 for his clear water picture
- Paladium for 'Ophannin Throne wheel of eyes ezekiel (with flame)'
- Adam Ognisty

I also acknowledge the following songwriters for their songs that have touched my heart and have been referred to in this book:
- Townend, Stuart – How deep the Father's love for us by https://creativecommons.org/licenses/by-sa/3.0/
- Cleland Boyd McAfee (September 25, 1866 – February 4, 1944) - Near to the heart of God
- Reginald Heber (21 April 1783 – 3 April 1826) - Holy, Holy, Holy
- Isaac Watts, 1674-1748 with Chorus by Ralph E. Hudson, 1843-1901 - At The Cross
- By Cortese Sisters (1975) - Love was when God became a man
- Frederick M. Lehman, (7 Aug 1868 - 20 Feb 1953) v. 3 by Anonymous/Unknown (1917) - The love of God

Foreword 1 – Pastor Austin Makota

Linda has once again demystified this book of prophetic symbols. In her first volume, she runs parallel with the Prophet and shows what he was shown in today's world. However, in Volume 2, Linda not only breaks down the hidden message but paints the picture and unveils with great accuracy the meanings, the times, and phenomena of this book. Her summation of both the Old Testament with the book of Revelation clearly shows us how God is behind this great book. This volume will not only open your eyes to the word but your heart as well. She makes it clear in her writing that God wants to move from the era of visitation to that of habitation. As you read this, the Veil will be removed from your eyes forever.

Be blessed.

Enjoy it.

Shalom

Pastor Austin Makota
Senior Pastor Bread of Life Church International

Foreword 2 – Reverend Carl Palmer

The book of Revelation is a daunting book. It generates more anxiety amongst Christians than any other part of scripture. What are we to make of its description of living creatures, locusts like horses, Seven bowls of wrath, war in heaven, various beasts, and a dragon?

But what if the Revelation of Jesus Christ is simply that, a revelation of Jesus Christ given from Jesus himself?

'The revelation from Jesus Christ, which God gave him to show his servants what must soon take place' Revelation 1:1

If I am one of his servants, then this message is for me, and for you too, the reader of this book.

Linda has a passion to teach, and God has clearly led her to communicate the gospel of Jesus Christ contained within the pages of this revelation. Rather than just being about future 'end of the world' type events this message is deeply relevant to our present age, and to followers of Jesus Christ in every age. God is on the throne, and he is ruling the universe. Linda has communicated the book of Revelation's deep truths in a way that is easily accessible to every reader without having to have a theological education. The book contains practical teaching from the scripture which we can apply into our everyday life right now.

'Blessed is the one who reads aloud the words of this prophecy, and blessed are those who hear it and take to heart what is written in it, because the time is near.' Revelation 1:3

It's not what we know, but what we do with what we know that ultimately counts. A blessing awaits you and I for not only reading Jesus' revelation, but for putting into practice it's message and living it out as his followers wherever we live, work or play.

May God bless us all.

Rev. Carl Palmer
The Baptist Union of Great Britain

Foreword 3 – Pastor Humphrey Walters

Here in this brief volume, Linda Green brings into sharp focus Revelation's key message: there's unstoppable hope for one and all! From years of careful research and reflection, she sets out to show how this oft misunderstood and misinterpreted Bible book fully supports this upbeat conclusion.

Even though wrong and evil seem, so often, to get the upper hand, good and right win out in the end. How so? From the command centre of our universe ('Mission Control', as Linda terms it here), Jesus is orchestrating his cosmic, climactic victory for the benefit of all.

Based upon a collection of her past sermons arising from this time-honoured text, she zeroes in on key insights from the Bible chapters herein reviewed (Revelation 4 and 5). Here we engage with insights, themes and applications that intersect with some of the most compelling issues of the day —our identity and destiny; our place and purpose in this world; why society's the way it is; how we can successfully navigate through the challenges of the present, as well as those that lie ahead of us, plus others. What's more, also included here are brief prayers and gospel songs (both old and new) to make this volume a choice devotional resource.

Not only is this a publication for the full-on Christian devotee, its general, non-technical style also ensures that it's likely to be hugely accessible for open-minded folk who live outside religious circles. Indeed, wherever readers might be coming from—the assembly line, the office, the hospital ward, the bank, the restaurant, the school, university or construction site etc—this publication will certainly provide help in the age-long quest for truth, certainty and meaning.

Pastor Humphrey Walters
Seventh-day Adventist Church

Introduction

So here I am writing *The Revelations of Jesus, Mission Control,* Volume Two. If you have read Volume One, you will know that this was not a venture I had in mind for myself, but the LORD moving in mysterious ways, has been taking me on a journey, and I am pleased to share it with you.

This time I am covering Revelation 4 and 5, two incredibly rich and enlightening chapters in the book of Revelation. I have called this Volume Mission Control because these Chapters deal with government from the throne of God and the Inauguration of Jesus Christ.

Again, I must say that whilst there are other ways to look at the apocalypse text, I look at Revelation from a historicist perspective.

I am amazed at the revelation of God's love for humanity in these chapters and I hope that you enjoy it as much as I have and that it grows your love for God and your faith in Him.

May God's love enthral you and fill you with joy and peace.

Linda Green

Revelation 4 - Mission Control (part one)

In Volume One of this series, we spent time looking at the revelations of Jesus to John in Revelation 1, 2, and 3 of the Bible. We learned that Jesus has been with His church from its beginning to the present day, whatever the circumstances or its functioning, and that Jesus will continue to be with the church until the end of the world.

I should clarify that Christ's church comprises believers through the ages and is not confined to any particular Christian denomination. We as individuals make up the church, and the messages apply to believers individually and collectively.

This account is entitled Mission Control. It is Jesus' revelation of the governance of His Father in heaven.

So, let's have a look at what is revealed.

Revelation 4:1 (NIV) The Throne in Heaven

> **4** After this I looked, and there before me was a door standing open in heaven. And the voice I had first heard speaking to me like a trumpet said, "Come up here, and I will show you what must take place after this."

John tells us at the start of Chapter 4 that he was called by the same voice that called him in Chapter 1. We established before that John described the Son of Man, our Lord and Saviour Jesus Christ, in Revelation Chapter 1 as the one who spoke to him. So, this invitation to enter the open door in heaven is from Jesus.

Before I continue, I would like to highlight some remarkable allusions in *Revelation 4:1*.

You may remember that in *Revelation 1:12, 13*, John saw Jesus walking amongst the lampstands; now, in *Revelation 4:1*, John sees an open door.

Interestingly, in the daily services of the sanctuary, after lots were cast and the officiating priest was selected,[1] one of the priest's first duties was to service the lampstand, replenish its oil, trim the wicks but ensure that the light of the lampstand never goes out.[2] The sanctuary lamp was often referred to as the 'eternal flame'.[3] The selected priest would attend to the table of shewbread and the altar of incense as well. When he finished the work in the Holy Place, he would open the sanctuary door to signal to the officiating priest that the daily sacrifices of the sin and burnt offerings could be made.[4]

Everything in the Holy Place represented the work of the Holy Spirit outside of heaven in God's people or believers. Everything in the Most Holy Place represented work in heaven. Everything outside in the courtyard illustrated work done for the salvation of humanity.

When we think about what Christ reveals with these symbols of the ministry of the church, it is a remarkable piece of imagery. Christ empowers His church or His people with the Holy Spirit, represented by the blazing lamps, and attends to their needs with spiritual provision and answered prayers. The open door represents that the ministry of salvation can begin.

What is that ministry?

That ministry is sharing the gospel of Christ, the Saviour of the world who came to earth and gave His life up in our stead. He took on our sins, known and unknown; He took on our sinfulness and gave us His righteousness. All who accept the gift of Salvation, a gift of love from God, purchased with the blood of His son Jesus Christ, will be saved!

---

[1] CRC, "The Sanctuary Service", Internet cited on 16.11.2021 at: https://www.crcbermuda.com/bible/the-sanctuary/the-sanctuary-service/chapter-11-the-daily-service
[2] Wikipedia, "Sanctuary Lamp", Internet cited on 16.11.2021 at: https://en.wikipedia.org/wiki/Sanctuary_lamp
[3] Ibid.
[4] Sefaria, "Mishnah Tamid", 3:2, Internet cited on 16.11.2021 at: https://www.sefaria.org/Mishnah_Tamid.1.1?lang=bi

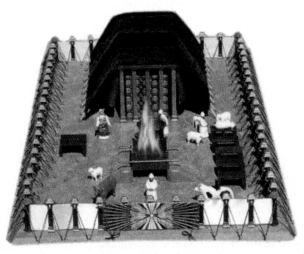

5

A representation of the Ancient Tabernacle

Below is an illustration of what it looked like inside the Holy Place and the Most Holy Place.

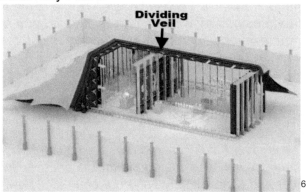

6

---

5 YAHUSHUA HA MASHIACH) THE CHIEF CORNERSTONE Ministry Congregation, Glasgow (Scotland, U.K.) "The "MISHKAN/Tabernacle of Moshe/Moses", Internet cited on 28.12.21 at: https://yahushua-thechiefcornerstone.com/the-tabernacle-of-moshe-moses/
6 The Bible Says, "Exodus 40:1-16", Internet cited on 17.11.2021 at: https://thebiblesays.com/commentary/exod/exod-40/exodus-401-16/

Jesus invites John to come and see.

Revelation 4:2-11

> *² At once I was in the Spirit, and there before me was a throne in heaven with someone sitting on it. ³ And the one who sat there had the appearance of jasper and ruby. A rainbow that shone like an emerald encircled the throne. ⁴ Surrounding the throne were twenty-four other thrones, and seated on them were twenty-four elders. They were dressed in white and had crowns of gold on their heads. ⁵ From the throne came flashes of lightning, rumblings and peals of thunder. In front of the throne, seven lamps were blazing. These are the seven spirits[sevenfold spirit]of God. ⁶ Also in front of the throne there was what looked like a sea of glass, clear as crystal.*
>
> *In the center, around the throne, were four living creatures, and they were covered with eyes, in front and in back. ⁷ The first living creature was like a lion, the second was like an ox, the third had a face like a man, the fourth was like a flying eagle. ⁸ Each of the four living creatures had six wings and was covered with eyes all around, even under its wings. Day and night, they never stop saying:*
>
> > *"'Holy, holy, holy*
> > *is the Lord God Almighty,*
> > *who was, and is, and is to come!"*
>
> *⁹ Whenever the living creatures give glory, honour and thanks to him who sits on the throne and who lives for ever and ever, ¹⁰ the twenty-four elders fall down before him who sits on the throne and worship him who lives for ever and ever. They lay their crowns before the throne and say:*
>
> > *¹¹ "You are worthy, our Lord and God,*
> > *to receive glory and honour and power,*
> > *for you created all things,*
> > *and by your will they were created and have their being."*

| Jasper | Ruby |

John tells us immediately he was in the spirit and entered the open door. That means he saw things as if he was there. John then describes what he saw. He is in the throne room of heaven and God is on the throne. John refers to God as "one who sat on the throne". He describes the appearance of God as like a jasper and ruby.

John does not describe God's face. Why does he only see God as shaped like a man the colour of jasper or ruby? The answer is found in *Exodus 33:18-20.*

> Then Moses said, "Now show me your glory."
>
> [19] *And the* LORD *said, "I will cause all my goodness to pass in front of you, and I will proclaim my name, the* LORD, *in your presence. I will have mercy on whom I will have mercy, and I will have compassion on whom I will*

---

[7] Wikimedia Commons, Dororenko (18 June 2010) "File:2010 - red jasper.jpg", Internet cited on 16.11.2021 at:
https://commons.wikimedia.org/wiki/File:2010_-_red_jasper.jpg
[8] Wikimedia Commons, Lavinsky, Robert M, (March 2010) "File:Corundum-215330.jpg", Internet cited on 16.11.2021 at:
https://commons.wikimedia.org/wiki/File:Corundum-215330.jpg

have compassion. **²⁰** *But," he said, "you cannot see my face, for no one may see me and live."*

²² *When my glory passes by, I will put you in a cleft in the rock and cover you with my hand until I have passed by.* **²³** *Then I will remove my hand and you will see my back; but my face must not be seen."*

Around the throne, there is a rainbow that shines like an emerald.

The rainbow is reminiscent of God's promise to Noah after the flood found in *Genesis 8:12-15.* You can read the story of the Flood in *Genesis chapters 6-9.* It is God's reminder of His promise to Noah and his family, His commitment to humanity.

Genesis 8:12-15 says,

> **¹²** *And God said, "This is the sign of the covenant I am making between me and you and every living creature with you, a covenant for all generations to come:* **¹³** *I have set my rainbow in the clouds, and it will be the sign of the*

¹¹ Wikimedia Commons, Geni (July 2018) "File: Duke of Devonshire Emerald.JPG", Internet cited on 16.11.2021 at: https://commons.wikimedia.org/wiki/File:Duke_of_Devonshire_Emerald.JPG

*covenant between me and the earth. ¹⁴ Whenever I bring
clouds over the earth and the rainbow appears in the
clouds, ¹⁵ I will remember my covenant between me and
you and all living creatures of every kind. Never again will
the waters become a flood to destroy all life.*

The Apostle John is given a view of what I call 'Mission Control'
of the universe. It is the place of government where God's law
and mercy work together for the good of the universe.[12]

Revelation 4:4

*⁴ Surrounding the throne were twenty-four other thrones,
and seated on them were twenty-four elders. They were
dressed in white and had crowns of gold on their heads.*

These twenty-four elders are not mentioned anywhere in the Old
Testament, but here they are in Revelation.

Around God's throne are twenty-four thrones on which sit twenty-
four elders, who are dressed in white. We know white garments
are a symbol of purity or righteousness. In scripture a crown
denotes rulership, but we don't know where these rulers are
from. These elders, rule in righteousness and holiness and are
seen around the throne of God.

We have an example of gatherings in the heavenly courts in *Job
1:6.7 (KJV)* which says,

*⁶ Now there was a day when the sons of God came to
present themselves before the LORD, and Satan came
also among them.*

---

[12] White, Ellen (13 December 1892) *The Review and Herrald,* par 7,
Internet on cited 16.11.21 at:
https://m.egwwritings.org/en/book/821.12368

> *⁷ And the LORD said unto Satan, whence comest thou?
> Then Satan answered the LORD, and said, From going to
> and fro in the earth, and from walking up and down in it.*

Adam is referred to as a son of God (*Genesis 6:2*) because God
made him, so these sons of God in Job are also God's creations.
They may be rulers of other worlds God has created.

Since subjugating Adam by causing him to sin, Satan saw
himself as the ruler of the earth, so he went to the assembly as
the representative of earth.

Perhaps John is being shown a heavenly council[13] where
decisions are made regarding the leadership of the universe.

Revelation 4:5, first part

> *⁵ From the throne came flashes of lightning, rumblings
> and peals of thunder. ...*

From the throne that God is sitting on, John hears loud and
attention-grabbing sounds! Flashes of lightning, rumblings and
peals of thunder.

Ezekiel also had a vision of heaven, and he says in **Ezekiel 1:14**

> *¹⁴ The creatures sped back and forth like flashes of
> lightning.*

The Psalmist said in **Psalms 29:3,4 and 7**

> *³ The voice of the LORD is over the waters;
>   the God of glory thunders,
>   the LORD thunders over the mighty waters.
> ⁴ The voice of the LORD is powerful;
>   the voice of the LORD is majestic.
> ⁷ The voice of the LORD strikes
>   with flashes of lightning.*

---

[13] Peckham, John C, (2018) *Theodicy of Love; Cosmic Conflict and the Problem of Evil,* Baker Academic, USA

I imagine that God is communicating with those around him in Mission Control. His voice sounds like thunder as He commands, and the creatures are moving like flashes of lightning to fulfil God's direction.

Revelation 4:5 last part

> *⁵ In front of the throne, seven lamps were blazing. These are the seven spirits [seven-fold spirit of God] of God.*

We know that the number seven represents perfection, so the seven-fold spirit is God's perfect spirit, aka **The Holy Spirit**. The lampstands we know from **Revelation 1:20** are the churches, so now the churches are represented as having the Holy Spirit and are before the throne of God.

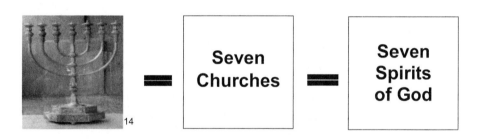

These symbols of the churches refer to us, the believers and messengers of the gospel, throughout the ages on the earth. The lamps are blazing, shining brightly before the throne of God because they are filled with the Spirit of God. They represent the Christian church tasked with spreading the gospel through the ages, assisted by the Holy Spirit.

I don't know if you got that. In Mission Control of the universe, God the Father is seated on His throne, and in front of His

---

¹⁴ Wikipedia Commons "File: Menorah 0307.jpg", Internet cited on 01.09.2021 at: https://commons.wikimedia.org/wiki/File:Menorah_0307.jpg

throne, right at the centre of the action, the churches' work on earth is represented by the blazing lamps.

As a Christian, I am overjoyed by this symbolism because it tells me that of all that God governs, of all that is going on in the universe, John is shown that the salvation of humans is central to the Kingdom of God. Our salvation is of primary importance to God. The church is of the highest importance to God. She is kept close to Him.

Revelation 4:6 (first part)

> [6] Also in front of the throne there was what looked like a sea of glass, clear as crystal.

Pilots refer to a perfectly still sea as a sea of glass. The sky is perfectly reflected in the still water, and it is difficult for them to see the horizon.

In front of the throne is a transparent, clear-as-crystal, and calm sea or expanse of water.

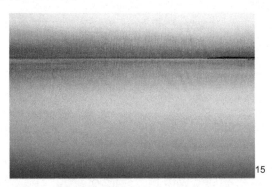
15

Revelation 4:6 (last part) – 8

> [6] In the center, around the throne, were four living creatures, and they were covered with eyes, in front and

[15] Photo by Harli Marten on Unsplash, Internet cited on 05.03.2023, at: https://unsplash.com/photos/n7a2OJDSZns

*in back. [7] The first living creature was like a lion, the
second was like an ox, the third had a face like a man,
the fourth was like a flying eagle. [8]Each of the four living
creatures had six wings and was covered with eyes all
around, even under its wings. Day and night, they never
stop saying:*

"Holy, holy, holy
is the Lord God Almighty,'
who was, and is, and is to come!"

In front of the throne are four living creatures with faces like a
lion, an ox, a man, and a flying eagle, each with six wings.

> C Mervyn Maxwell proposes that the lion's head portrays
> the creature's strength, whilst the ox symbolises willing
> service, the eagle represents swiftness and
> perceptiveness, and the human face represents
> intelligence.[16]

The four living creatures have eyes all over them. So, there is no
direction that they cannot see. They have 360° vision. They can
see in every direction at all times. They have global vision.

John's vision shows that God's church, filled with His Holy Spirit,
is of utmost importance to God. God's church is you and I, the
believers, who have accepted His gift of salvation. He keeps us
close.

Just like the arrangements for seating guests at a royal banquet,
the most important people are placed nearest to the monarch.
So, you and I are most important to God and are placed next to
Him in the throne room vision.

---

[16] Maxwell C. Mervyn (1985) *God Cares, Vol 2: The Message of
Revelation for you and your family,* Pacific Publishing Association,
Ontario, Canada, p.153.

An artist's impression of what John saw in Revelation 4.

17

***

17 Used with permission. Art by © 2022 McKenzie Blaze

Song:

Near to the heart of God
By Cleland Boyd McAfee (September 25, 1866 – February 4, 1944)

There is a place of quiet rest,
near to the heart of God,
a place where sin cannot molest,
near to the heart of God.

Refrain:
O Jesus, blest Redeemer,
sent from the heart of God,
hold us, who wait before thee,
near to the heart of God.

There is a place of comfort sweet,
near to the heart of God,
a place where we our Saviour meet,
near to the heart of God. [Refrain]

There is a place of full release,
near to the heart of God,
a place where all is joy and peace,
near to the heart of God. [Refrain]

Prayer

Dear God of the universe, thank you for caring so much about us that you keep us close to you. Help us to find the comfort, joy and peace that comes from you, in Jesus' name.

Amen

Revelation 4: Mission Control (part two)

Revelation 4:6 (last part) – 8

> *6 In the center, around the throne, were four living creatures, and they were covered with eyes, in front and in back. 7 The first living creature was like a lion, the second was like an ox, the third had a face like a man, the fourth was like a flying eagle. 8Each of the four living creatures had six wings and was covered with eyes all around, even under its wings. Day and night, they never stop saying:*
>
> > *"Holy, holy, holy*
> > *is the Lord God Almighty,'*
> > *who was, and is, and is to come!"*

In the Old Testament, Ezekiel has two visions of heaven's Mission Control, in which he describes four creatures.

Ezekiel is 30 years old and is with the Israelite exiles in Babylon when he gets his first vision.

Ezekiel 1:4-11

> *4 I looked, and I saw a windstorm coming out of the north—an immense cloud with flashing lightning and surrounded by brilliant light. The center of the fire looked like glowing metal, 5 and in the fire was what looked like four living creatures. In appearance their form was human, 6 but each of them had four faces and four wings. 7 Their legs were straight; their feet were like those of a calf and gleamed like burnished bronze. 8 Under their wings on their four sides they had human hands. All four of them had faces and wings, 9 and the wings of one touched the wings of another. Each one went straight ahead; they did not turn as they moved. 10 Their faces looked like this: Each of the four had the face of a human being, and on the right side each had the face of a lion,*

*and on the left the face of an ox; each also had the face
of an eagle. ⁱⁱ Such were their faces.
They each had two wings spreading out upward, each
wing touching that of the creature on either side; and
each had two other wings covering its body.*

Notice these are the same faces, Ezekiel sees the same faces
and each creature has four faces and four wings. It is
reminiscent of John's vision but he saw each creature with one
face.

Ezekiel 1:12-16

*¹² Each one went straight ahead. Wherever the spirit
would go, they would go, without turning as they went. ¹³
The appearance of the living creatures was like burning
coals of fire or like torches. Fire moved back and forth
among the creatures; it was bright, and lightning flashed
out of it. ¹⁴ The creatures sped back and forth like flashes
of lightning.*

18

*¹⁵ As I looked at the living creatures, I saw a wheel on the
ground beside each creature with its four faces. ¹⁶ This
was the appearance and structure of the wheels: They
sparkled like topaz, and all four looked alike. Each
appeared to be made like a wheel intersecting a wheel.*

---

¹⁸ VoiceTube, "Ezekiel's Astonishing Vision of God", Internet cited on
17.11.2021 at: https://www.voicetube.com/videos/78522

[19]

Ezekiel then describes their movement, the creatures and their wheels working together, following the direction of God.

Ezekiel 1:17-21

> *[17] As they moved, they would go in any one of the four directions the creatures faced; the wheels did not change direction as the creatures went. [18] Their rims were high and awesome, and all four rims were full of eyes all around.*
>
> *[19] When the living creatures moved, the wheels beside them moved; and when the living creatures rose from the ground, the wheels also rose. [20] Wherever the spirit would go, they would go, and the wheels would rise along with them, because the spirit of the living creatures was in the wheels. [21] When the creatures moved, they also moved; when the creatures stood still, they also stood still; and when the creatures rose from the ground, the wheels rose along with them, because the spirit of the living creatures was in the wheels.*

---

[19] Used with permission ©McKenzieBlaze deb 2022.

Ezekiel 1:22-26

22 *Spread out above the heads of the living creatures was what looked something like a vault, sparkling like crystal, and awesome.* 23 *Under the vault their wings were stretched out one toward the other, and each had two wings covering its body.* 24 *When the creatures moved, I heard the sound of their wings, like the roar of rushing waters, like the voice of the Almighty, like the tumult of an army. When they stood still, they lowered their wings.*

25 *Then there came a voice from above the vault over their heads as they stood with lowered wings.* 26 *Above the vault over their heads was what looked like a throne of lapis lazuli, and high above on the throne was a figure like that of a man.*

[20]

[20] Wikimedia Commons, "File:1 lapis lazuli.jpg", Internet cited on 17.11.2021 at:
https://commons.wikimedia.org/wiki/File:1_lapis_lazuli.jpg

Ezekiel sees what John saw, but he sees the images in a hierarchical symbolism where God is on top, and everything is below Him, but John saw the symbols in a circular form where God is at the centre. Both are the same thing, expressed differently.

Ezekiel describes God's throne as like lapis lazuli, in other words, a bright blue colour.

God is further described *in **Ezekiel 1: 27-28,***

> *27 I saw that from what appeared to be his waist up he looked like glowing metal, as if full of fire, and that from there down he looked like fire; and brilliant light surrounded him. 28 Like the appearance of a rainbow in the clouds on a rainy day, so was the radiance around him.*
>
> *This was the appearance of the likeness of the glory of the LORD. When I saw it, I fell facedown, and I heard the voice of one speaking.*

22

Later, Ezekiel has another vision of the four creatures. Much of the description is as in Ezekiel 1, and Revelation 4.

In **Ezekiel 10:5** Ezekiel calls the creatures Cherubim.

> *⁵ The sound of the wings of the cherubim could be heard as far away as the outer court, like the voice of God Almighty when he speaks.*

In **Ezekiel 10:20-22**, he says,

> *²⁰ These were the living creatures I had seen beneath the God of Israel by the Kebar River, and I realized that they were cherubim. ²¹ Each had four faces and four wings, and under their wings was what looked like human hands. ²² Their faces had the same appearance as those I had seen by the Kebar River. Each one went straight ahead.*

What John and Ezekiel saw are similar but different. So, what is going on?

Let's have a look at **Exodus 25:18-20 (NIV)**

> *¹⁸ And make two cherubim out of hammered gold at the ends of the cover. ¹⁹ Make one cherub on one end and the second cherub on the other; make the cherubim of one piece with the cover, at the two ends. ²⁰ The cherubim are to have their wings spread upward, overshadowing the cover with them. The cherubim are to face each other, looking toward the cover.*

The cherubim that cover over the covenant ark were made from one piece of hammered gold. One cherub on either end of the cover with their wings joined, like the wings of the creatures who carry out God's biddings, working together and moving in unison.

Ezekiel was a priest and had been inside the temple, so he recognised the cherubim.

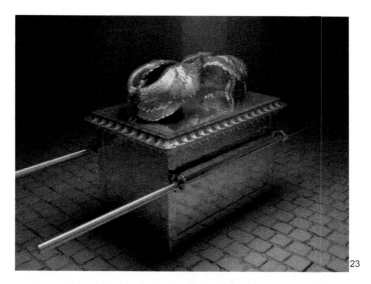

²³

In the Most Holy place of the tabernacle and the temple, above the ark, the cooperative work between God and the cherubim on behalf of humanity was represented on the ark. The ark was placed in the innermost part of the sanctuary. It described the work directed by God in heaven. The Most Holy place was where the high priest, who represented Jesus, received directions and communicated with God.

Numbers 7:89 (NIV)

> [89] When Moses entered the tent of meeting to speak with the LORD, he heard the voice speaking to him from between the two cherubim above the atonement cover on the ark of the covenant law. In this way the LORD spoke to him.

John and Ezekiel were shown the same work, symbolically.

The impressive wheels of the cherubim are said to be the spirit of the cherubim. (*Ezekiel 1:20*)

---

[23] Free Bible Images, "The ark of the covenant", Internet cited on 09.06.2022 at: https://www.freebibleimages.org/illustrations/bs-ark-covenant/

The word translated spirit is **ruwach (pronounced ru akh),** meaning **essence or life/breath**.

The wheels reach the earth and are covered with eyes, as are the cherubim, so they see everything and are ever moving forward in whatever direction they go. These beings symbolised the work angels do on earth, directed by God the Father.

From Ezekiel, we learn that the four creatures are cherubim. Cherub is the singular noun.

The cherubim/creatures/angels, like flashes of lightning, go to and fro, fulfilling God's directions and serving humanity's needs. They see everything. As they move their wings, they sound like the voice of God.

John and Ezekiel's visions are similar but different because what they are shown are symbols of God's work in heaven and earth on our behalf.

Throughout the Bible, we have evidence of the work the angels of God do in our world.

In *Genesis 28:12,* Jacob dreams of a ladder/stairway between heaven and earth, and the angels of God were ascending and descending on it. This dream was also symbolic of the work of angels on earth, directed by God the Father.

Jesus spoke about angels during His time on earth. (See Apendix 1)

In the ancient world, God expressed His salvatory work in the symbols of the sanctuary.

Exodus 25:8,9 (NIV)

> [8]*"Then have them make a sanctuary for me, and I will dwell among them. [9] Make this tabernacle and all its furnishings exactly like the pattern I will show you.*

The sanctuary was physical evidence that God was not distant; He lived amongst His people.

Exodus 26:1, 31 (NIV)

The Tabernacle

> [1] *"Make the tabernacle with ten curtains of finely twisted linen and blue, purple and scarlet yarn, with cherubim woven into them by a skilled worker.*
>
> [31] *"Make a curtain of blue, purple and scarlet yarn and finely twisted linen, with cherubim woven into it by a skilled worker.*

This curtain was the inner covering of the sanctuary as the Israelites travelled through the wilderness until Solomon built the temple. The inner cover was embroidered with cherubim to show the work of angels with God's people here on earth as directed by God in heaven.

We have seen that the ark of the covenant, which was placed in the Most Holy part of the temple, had two cherubim on its Atonement Cover (Mercy seat, according to KJV Bible). Two of the cherubims' wings touched each other, and their other wings covered their body. The cherubim and the atonement lid of the Ark were made of one piece of gold to symbolise these angels' cooperative work as they actively carried out God's commands.

Curtains divided the Holy section and the Most Holy section of the tabernacle, decorated with cherubim.

The objects in the Most Holy place represented the work in heaven. God is in heaven, but He directs the heavenly hosts to act in response to our prayers. The objects in the Holy place represented the work of God amongst believers. God's Holy Spirit works amongst His church, represented by the lighted lampstands. The prayers of the saints represented by the incense burning on the altar rise daily to God, who responds, and the table of shewbread represents God's provision for our needs and our gratitude for His benevolence towards us. The objects in the courtyard represented the work of salvation for the whole world, for humanity. It represents the world into which Jesus came and died for the sins of all men to make salvation available to all.

Everything in the tabernacle represented aspects of God's work on our behalf.

In ancient times, there was no Bible for people to read. What they knew about God came through oral recitals passed down through the generations and whatever the spiritual leaders taught the people.

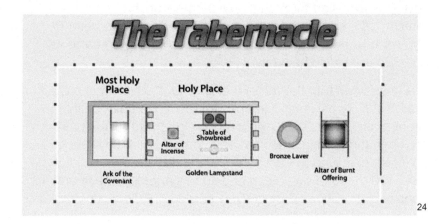

24

Let's have a look at how God led Israel.

Exodus 25:21-22

> [21] Place the cover on top of the ark and put in the ark the tablets of the covenant law that I will give you. [22] There, above the cover between the two cherubim that are over

24 Circe Institute, Phillips, Brian (30th May 2017) "A walk through the Tabernacle", Internet cited on 26.11.2021 at: https://www.pngkit.com/downpic/u2q8y3o0a9o0r5u2_layout-of-the-tabernacle-tabernacle-dimensions/

the ark of the covenant law, I will meet with you and give you all my commands for the Israelites.

Numbers 7:89

> [89] *When Moses entered the tent of meeting to speak with the LORD, he heard the voice speaking to him from between the two cherubim above the atonement cover on the ark of the covenant law. In this way the LORD spoke to him.*

The Shekinah glory of the Lord came between the space above the Atonement cover (Mercy Seat), and the overarched wings of the cherubim. The priests heard the voice of the Lord from there.

We learnt from Ezekiel that the cherubim work in unison, carrying out the commands of God in heaven and on earth. They move as swift as lightning, and it is through them that God's voice is heard.

---

[25] Eye of Prophecy, Garybowers, (27 June 2015) "The Ark of the Covenant...Part II", Internet cited on 18.11.2021 at:
https://eyeofprophecy.com/2015/06/27/the-ark-of-the-covenant-part-ii/

As they carry out the work of God, they are filled with love, awe, and appreciation for God's incredible love and mercy.

Revelation 4:9-11

> [9] *Whenever the living creatures give glory, honour and thanks to him who sits on the throne and who lives for ever and ever,* [10] *the twenty-four elders fall down before him who sits on the throne and worship him who lives for ever and ever. They lay their crowns before the throne and say:*
> [11] *"You are worthy, our Lord and God,*
> *to receive glory and honour and power,*
> *for you created all things,*
> *and by your will they were created and have their being."*

The four living cherubim and the twenty-four elders respond to God's mercy and judgement by calling, *"Holy, Holy, Holy! Lord God Almighty!"*

The cherubim qualify their call with the reason for their exclamation.

In John's vision, the creatures cry, "Who was, who is and is to come!" In other words, God is, was, and will always be God! Who, by His will, created and brought into existence all that live! There is no one like Him. He is eternal, and His judgements and actions cause the heavenly beings to exclaim their praises, fall down, and worship him.

The living creatures and the twenty-four elders are overwhelmed by His love and mercy and by God's judgements and actions for the good of humanity that they exclaim their praises continually as they do their work. These are not passive, geed-up, semi-conscious sets of individuals calling out senselessly. These are beings involved in the work of our salvation, and their responses to God's directions are ones of awe and praise.

The twenty-four elders throw off their crowns, not in abdication but in submission and recognition that they are subject to

Almighty God who is worthy of rulership. They are righteous rulers themselves, but in God's presence, they feel humbled. They fall on their faces, throwing off their crowns to give homage and honour to the most just, the most loving, the most merciful God, the one who sits on the throne of the cosmos.

Despite the vast expanse of the cosmos that God actively supports, Revelation 4 show us that God the Father is primarily active in our salvation. He is intensely interested in us and our well-being, now and for eternity. We are **priority number one**.

I don't know about you, but I am grateful that the God of heaven loves us so much that **we are central to His directions** in the courts of heaven. We are priority number one.

We can join the creatures and elders in praising a God who loves us so much that His primary focus is our salvation

***

Song:

Holy, Holy, Holy
By Reginald Heber (21 April 1783 – 3 April 1826)

1 Holy, holy, holy! Lord God Almighty!
Early in the morning our song shall rise to thee.
Holy, holy, holy, merciful and mighty!
God in three persons, blessed Trinity!

2 Holy, holy, holy! All the saints adore thee,
casting down their golden crowns around the glassy sea;
cherubim and seraphim falling down before thee,
which wert and art and evermore shalt be.

3 Holy, holy, holy! Though the darkness hide thee,
though the eye of sinful man thy glory may not see,
only thou art holy; there is none beside thee,
perfect in power, in love, and purity.

4 Holy, holy, holy! Lord God Almighty!
All thy works shall praise thy name
in earth, and sky and sea.
Holy, holy, holy! merciful and mighty!

Prayer

O God, our God, how excellent is your name in all the earth!
How can we sufficiently thank you for your goodness towards
us?
Help us O Lord to seek you and to serve you in love and
appreciation of your love for us. May we dwell in your presence
always. In Jesus' name.

Amen

Revelation 5: Mission Control (part three)

Revelation 5:1-5 (NIV)

The Scroll and the Lamb

> **5** *Then I saw in the right hand of him who sat on the throne a scroll with writing on both sides and sealed with seven seals.* *² And I saw a mighty angel proclaiming in a loud voice, "Who is worthy to break the seals and open the scroll?"* *³ But no one in heaven or on earth or under the earth could open the scroll or even look inside it.* *⁴ I wept and wept because no one was found who was worthy to open the scroll or look inside.* *⁵ Then one of the elders said to me, "Do not weep! See, the Lion of the tribe of Judah, the Root of David, has triumphed. He is able to open the scroll and its seven seals."*

God the Father, is on His throne and has a scroll in His right hand.

Perhaps if the vision was today, God might have been holding a book or a tablet, or e-reader, something we would recognise as holding records or information.

The information is sealed/or safeguarded. If the vision were in our time, it would have seven layers of authentication/verification so that it can only be opened by an individual who qualifies or is authorised to do so.

What is the significance of the scroll?

To find out, we need to look at Ancient Israel.

In *1 Samuel 8*, the Israelites told Samuel they wanted a king to rule over them. Samuel is upset by their request, but God tells Samuel it wasn't him that Israel rejected; they were rejecting God. Samuel told them all that would happen if a man rules them, but the people still wanted a king. They wanted an earthly king to rule them when they already had the King of kings leading them.

After anointing Saul as the first King of Israel, Samuel summons the people and tells them what the practices and duties of a king of Israel would be.

1 Samuel 10:25 (NIV) tells us what was in the scroll.

> ²⁵ *Samuel explained to the people the rights and duties of kingship. He wrote them down on a scroll and deposited it before the LORD. Then Samuel dismissed the people to go to their own homes.*

What were those rights and duties?

To find out, let's read *Deuteronomy 17:14-20*

The King

> ¹⁴ *When you enter the land the LORD your God is giving you and have taken possession of it and settled in it, and you say, "Let us set a king over us like all the nations around us," ¹⁵ be sure to appoint over you a king the LORD your God chooses. He must be from among your fellow Israelites. Do not place a foreigner over you, one who is not an Israelite. ¹⁶ The king, moreover, must not acquire great numbers of horses for himself or make the people return to Egypt to get more of them, for the LORD has told you, "You are not to go back that way again." ¹⁷ He must not take many wives, or his heart will be led astray. He must not accumulate large amounts of silver and gold.*

> ¹⁸ *When he takes the throne of his kingdom, he is to write for himself on a scroll a copy of this law, taken from that of the Levitical priests. ¹⁹ It is to be with him, and he is to read it all the days of his life so that he may learn to revere the LORD his God and follow carefully all the words of this law and these decrees ²⁰ and not consider himself better than his fellow Israelites and turn from the law to*

the right or to the left. Then he and his descendants will reign a long time over his kingdom in Israel.

Note that this was told to Israel before they entered the Promised land. So, God knew they would reject Him as their leader, but He kept His covenant with Israel.

2 Kings 11:4-12 (NIV) tells the story of the inauguration of Joash as King of Judah

> *[4] In the seventh year Jehoiada sent for the commanders of units of a hundred, the Carites and the guards and had them brought to him at the temple of the LORD. He made a covenant with them and put them under oath at the temple of the LORD. Then he showed them the king's son. [5] He commanded them, saying, "This is what you are to do: You who are in the three companies that are going on duty on the Sabbath—a third of you guarding the royal palace, [6] a third at the Sur Gate, and a third at the gate behind the guard, who take turns guarding the temple— [7] and you who are in the other two companies that normally go off Sabbath duty are all to guard the temple for the king. [8] Station yourselves around the king, each of you with weapon in hand. Anyone who approaches your ranks is to be put to death. Stay close to the king wherever he goes."*
> *[9] The commanders of units of a hundred did just as Jehoiada the priest ordered. Each one took his men— those who were going on duty on the Sabbath and those who were going off duty—and came to Jehoiada the priest. [10] Then he gave the commanders the spears and shields that had belonged to King David and that were in the temple of the LORD. [11] The guards, each with weapon in hand, stationed themselves around the king—near the altar and the temple, from the south side to the north side of the temple. [12] Jehoiada brought out the king's son and put the crown on him; he presented him with a copy of the covenant and proclaimed him king. They anointed*

him, and the people clapped their hands and shouted,
"Long live the king!

The book of the covenant is the scroll Samuel had written. By accepting the scroll, the king was established as the people's religious leader and established on the royal throne.

In **Revelation 5:2**, when the mighty angel called out, *"Who is worthy to break the seals and open the scroll?"* A search ensues in heaven, on the earth and of those under the earth (those asleep until the resurrection); no one is found who is worthy. The search is for one who is worthy to rule. Someone worthy to lead the cosmos.

Revelation 5:3 says,

> *³ But no one in heaven or on earth or under the earth could open the scroll or even look inside it. ⁴ I wept and wept because no one was found who was worthy to open the scroll or look inside.*

There is no angel or cherub or human being, alive or dead, on the earth or in heaven who can open the scroll or look inside.

Pastor John Lomacang of 3ABN, in a discourse on this Bible passage, proposed that Jesus was on his way to heaven at the time of the search, following his death and resurrection. He was not on the earth and not yet in heaven. That is why no one is found worthy in heaven or on earth.

John begins to weep; he is distraught. He, like everyone else, is keen to know what God the Father has written down. As he weeps, one of the twenty-four elders speaks to him and says in

Revelation 5:5,

> *"Do not weep! See, the Lion of the tribe of Judah, the Root of David, has triumphed. He is able to open the scroll and its seven seals."*

Who is the Lion of the tribe of Judah?

In *Genesis 49:9-10,* Jacob blesses his son Judah before his death, and this is what he said to Judah.

Genesis 49: 9,10 (NIV)

> *⁹ You are a lion's cub, Judah;*
> *you return from the prey, my son.*
> *Like a lion he crouches and lies down,*
> *like a lioness—who dares to rouse him?*
> **¹⁰ The sceptre will not depart from Judah,**
> **nor the ruler's staff from between his feet,[a]**
> **until he to whom it belongs[b] shall come**
> **and the obedience of the nations shall be his.**

Footnotes:

a. Genesis 49:10 Or *from his descendants*
b. Genesis 49:10 Or *to whom tribute belongs*; the meaning of the Hebrew for this phrase is uncertain.

A descendant of Judah will be a ruler to whom the nations owe their obedience. This descendent is the Lion of the tribe or the ruler of all nations.

Matthew 1:1-16 traces Jesus the Messiah's genealogy from Abraham, through Abraham's great-grandson **Judah**, through the generations to King David of Israel, and then through further descendants until Joseph, husband of Mary, mother of Jesus.

When Philip the disciple asks Jesus in **John 14:8-11** to show them the Father, Jesus replied,

> *⁸ Anyone who has seen me has seen the Father. How can you say, 'Show us the Father'?*
> *¹⁰ Don't you believe that I am in the Father and that the Father is in me? The words I say to you I do not speak on*

*my own authority. Rather, it is the Father, living in me,
who is doing his work.*
*¹¹ Believe me when I say that I am in the Father and the
Father is in me;*

Jesus is saying to Philip when you see me; you see the Father.
We are the same. What I do, He does, what I say, He says. I am
everything that my Father is.

In **John 8:58**, Jesus says, speaking to the Jews,

> *⁵⁸ "Very truly I tell you," ..., "before Abraham was born,
> I Am!"*

As a human, Jesus is a descendent of Judah, the great-
grandson of Abraham, but He tells the Jews he existed before
Abraham. He uses a term the Jews recognised as belonging to
God when he said, "I Am!"

They knew that in their history, God had said this to Moses when
he asked God who shall I say has sent me?

Exodus 3:14 (NIV)

> *¹⁴ God said to Moses, "I am who I am. This is what you
> are to say to the Israelites: 'I am has sent me to you.'"*

Jesus was saying He is the I AM. He is the one that spoke to
Moses in the burning bush.

The Lion, or ruler, of the tribe of Judah that was to come is
Jesus.

The Root of David who existed before David and is of the lineage
of David is Jesus.

Jesus is the I AM. He is both God and man.

What John is being shown is an inauguration ceremony. Only
the rightful ruler can accept and open the scrolls in God's hands.

In **Revelation 5:5,** one of the twenty-four elders says to John,

> *"Do not weep! See, the Lion of the tribe of Judah, the Root of David, has triumphed. He is able to open the scroll and its seven seals."*

We know that this is Jesus. He has triumphed.

To triumph, you have to have been in a battle or contest and won.

What battle has Jesus been in?

Revelation 12:7-9 tells us

> *⁷ Then war broke out in heaven. Michael and his angels fought against the dragon, and the dragon and his angels fought back. ⁸ But he was not strong enough, and they lost their place in heaven. ⁹ The great dragon was hurled down—that ancient serpent called the devil, or Satan, who leads the whole world astray. He was hurled to the earth, and his angels with him.*

So, Satan, aka the devil, is defeated and has lost his place in heaven.

Who is Michael?

Michael means "one who is like God." [26]

In Daniel 10, Daniel has a vision that he does not understand. He prays for understanding, and an angel is sent to explain his vision to him. **Daniel 10:11-14, 20, 21 (NIVUK)**

> *¹¹ He said, 'Daniel, you who are highly esteemed, consider carefully the words I am about to speak to you, and stand up, for I have now been sent to you.' And when he said this to me, I stood up trembling.*

---

[26] Plant, Renee, (3rd July 2021) "Michael Name Meaning", Internet cited on 02.12.2021 at: https://www.verywellfamily.com/michael-name-meaning-5115812

[12] Then he continued, 'Do not be afraid, Daniel. Since the first day that you set your mind to gain understanding and to humble yourself before your God, your words were heard, and I have come in response to them. [13] But the prince of the Persian kingdom resisted me twenty-one days. Then Michael, one of the chief princes, came to help me, because I was detained there with the king of Persia. [14] Now I have come to explain to you what will happen to your people in the future, for the vision concerns a time yet to come.'

20 So he said, 'Do you know why I have come to you? Soon I will return to fight against the prince of Persia, and when I go, the prince of Greece will come; 21 but first I will tell you what is written in the Book of Truth.

The angel sent to Daniel identifies Michael as the **Chief Prince** and **Daniel's Prince,** who helps him fight the Prince of Persia.

In *Jude 1:9,* Michael is called the **Archangel,** who resurrects Moses and rebukes Satan.

Who has the ability to give life?

Only God can give life! So, the chief Prince, or Archangel, is Jesus.

Michael is the Chief of the angels, a Prince in the heavenly courts, and Daniel's Prince. He is Jesus.

When Jesus accepts the scroll in God's right hand, He accepts rulership over the universe.

In the ancient world, after a new king ascends the throne, enemies of the king are arrested and killed, or they are banished. We can read about what happened when Solomon was anointed king in 1 Kings 1, 2. His brother Adonijah who had assumed the kingship, and Joab, who supported Adonijah, were killed. Solomon gave them grace initially, but they continued to seek power and were killed as a result of their actions.

Those who were loyal to the king were rewarded.

Let's see what happens after Joash is inaugurated as King of Israel.

We need to go back a bit to get the background to what happens next.

2 Kings 11:1-3 tells of Athaliah's ascension to the throne.

Athaliah and Joash

11 When Athaliah the mother of Ahaziah saw that her son was dead, she proceeded to destroy the whole royal family. ² But Jehosheba, the daughter of King Jehoram and sister of Ahaziah, took Joash son of Ahaziah and stole him away from among the royal princes, who were about to be murdered. She put him and his nurse in a bedroom to hide him from Athaliah; so, he was not killed. ³ He remained hidden with his nurse at the temple of the LORD for six years while Athaliah ruled the land.

Athaliah was Joash's grandmother, but she was his enemy because had she known of his existence, she would have killed him.

Now let's look at *2 Kings 11:13-16*

¹³ When Athaliah heard the noise made by the guards and the people, she went to the people at the temple of the LORD. ¹⁴ She looked and there was the king, standing by the pillar, as the custom was. The officers and the trumpeters were beside the king, and all the people of the land were rejoicing and blowing trumpets. Then Athaliah tore her robes and called out, "Treason! Treason!"

¹⁵ Jehoiada the priest ordered the commanders of units of a hundred, who were in charge of the troops: "Bring her out between the ranks and put to the sword anyone who follows her." For the priest had said, "She must not be put

to death in the temple of the LORD." ^{16} *So they seized her as she reached the place where the horses enter the palace grounds, and there she was put to death.*

Athaliah was an enemy of the new king and threatened his position as king, so she was killed.

Let's go back to Revelation and see what happens at Jesus' inauguration.

In **Revelation 12:10** *(KJV),* we are told,

> *And I heard a loud voice saying in heaven, Now is come salvation, and strength, and the kingdom of our God, and the power of his Christ: for the **accuser** of our brethren is cast down, which accused them before our God day and night.*

Up to this time, Satan continuously accuses those who believe in Jesus before God, day and night. He could go in and out of the heavenly courts, claiming that he is the earth's rightful ruler because of our sin.

Satan constantly accused us and questioned God's judgement and motives concerning humans in heaven.

In the story of Job, we have a picture of Satan's activities on the earth and in heaven. Satan attends an assembly of the rulers of the various worlds as representative of the earth, where he believes he rules. God tells him that He has a faithful servant in Job. *(Job 1:6-2:1-10)*

At the cross, God the Father and Jesus allowed Satan the freedom to do as he wished.

The universe saw what Satan was really about, at the cross. Satan wanted Jesus dead.

Satan led the Pharisees and Priests, inspiring them to gee up the crowds in a frenzy, crying out, "Crucify Him! Crucify Him!"

Satan wanted Jesus dead, and God allowed him the freedom to kill His Son.

As a result, Satan could no longer enter heaven and stand accusing us before God. He had shown his true colours. He who Jesus created, was prepared to kill his Creator. The universe looked on in horror as the Saviour was beaten, abused and murdered. In doing so, Satan showed himself for what he was. Satan could no longer influence the beings of the cosmos, so he could no longer go to heaven and peddle his accusations and lies. Only here on earth can he deceive the people. Only here on earth can Satan peddle his lies.

Jesus won that day!

The wages of sin is death, but Jesus was not guilty of any sin. Instead, He took our guilt upon himself and died in our stead to give us the victory over sin.

At the Cross, Jesus won! He is worthy to accept and open the scroll.

Song:

At The Cross

Lyrics by Isaac Watts, 1674-1748
Chorus by Ralph E. Hudson, 1843-1901

1. Alas! and did my Savior bleed?
And did my Sov'reign die?
Would He devote that sacred head
For such a worm as I?

Chorus:
At the cross, at the cross,
Where I first saw the light,
And the burden of my heart rolled away -
It was there by faith I received my sight,
And now I am happy all the day.

2. Was it for crimes that I have done
He groaned upon the tree?
Amazing pity! Grace unknown!
And love beyond degree!

3. Well might the sun in darkness hide
And shut its glories in,
When Christ, the mighty Maker, died
For man the creature's sin.

4. Thus might I hide my blushing face
While His dear cross appears;
Dissolve my heart in thankfulness,
And melt mine eyes to tears.

5. But drops of grief can ne'er repay
The debt of love I owe:
Here, Lord, I give myself away -
'Tis all that I can do!

Prayer:

Oh God,

How can we say thanks for what you have done for us?
There are no words sufficient to convey our gratitude, and our
gratitude is small compared to the magnitude of what you have
done for us!

Thank you for your love, your mercy and your grace.
Thank you for loving us so much you would bear the shame and
disgrace of the cross on our behalf!

Thank you for paying the price for our sins so we can be free.
Thank you, thank you, thank you!

Amen.

Revelation 5: Mission Control (part four)

Revelation 5:5

> *5 Then one of the elders said to me, "Do not weep! See, the Lion of the tribe of Judah, the Root of David, has triumphed. He is able to open the scroll and its seven seals."*

The battle that started in heaven is not fought with swords and spears or guns and bombs.

It was not a cold war fought by missions of espionage. There was nothing that Satan had that God did not know about.

This battle is one of ideas, and a battle in which an angel, Lucifer, wanted to have the same position as God our Creator.

Isaiah 14:12-14 KJV

> *12 How art thou fallen from heaven, **O Lucifer** [light bearer**], son of the morning!** how art thou cut down to the ground, which didst weaken the nations!*
> *13 For thou hast said in thine heart, I will ascend into heaven, I will exalt my throne above the stars of God: I will sit also upon the mount of the congregation, in the sides of the north:*
> *14 I will ascend above the heights of the clouds; I will be like the Most High.*
> *15 Yet thou shalt be brought down to hell, to the sides of the pit.*

Only the King James Version of the Bible interprets the Greek as Lucifer, which means "light-bearer".

In the NIV, the translation is "morning star, son of the dawn".

A literal translation from Greek would say "Shining one, Son of the dawn".

Let's read about him in *Ezekiel 28:12-17 (NIV)*

¹² "Son of man, take up a lament concerning the king of
Tyre and say to him: 'This is what the
Sovereign LORD says:

"'You were the seal of perfection,
full of wisdom and perfect in beauty.
¹³ You were in Eden, the garden of God;
every precious stone adorned you:
carnelian, chrysolite and emerald,
topaz, onyx and jasper,
lapis lazuli, turquoise and beryl.[a]
Your settings and mountings[b] were made of gold;
    on the day you were created they were prepared.
¹⁴ You were anointed as a guardian cherub,
    for so I ordained you.
You were on the holy mount of God;
    you walked among the fiery stones.
¹⁵ You were blameless in your ways
    from the day you were created
    till wickedness was found in you.
¹⁶ Through your widespread trade
    you were filled with violence,
    and you sinned.
So I drove you in disgrace from the mount of God,
    and I expelled you, guardian cherub,
    from among the fiery stones.
¹⁷ Your heart became proud
    on account of your beauty,
and you corrupted your wisdom
    because of your splendor.
So I threw you to the earth;
    I made a spectacle of you before kings.

Footnotes

    a. Ezekiel 28:13 The precise identification of some of
       these precious stones is uncertain.
    b. Ezekiel 28:13 The meaning of the Hebrew for this
       phrase is uncertain.

The text is not talking about an earthly King of Tyre here. We know this because verse 13 says he was in the Garden of Eden. So, he was present in the newly made earth. The verse also lists his adornments. Verse 14 tells us who the text is talking about, a guardian cherub that God created, who was expelled from the mount of God because sin was found in his heart.

Lucifer, the Shining One, the Morning Star, was cast down to the earth because he wanted to occupy the place of God, but instead of ascending to worship and adoration of the heavenly court, he is cast to the earth.

Imagine for a moment that you are Lucifer, and you want to be worshipped. Everyone in heaven loves each other and loves and worships God wholeheartedly. The angels love you as well. After all, you are a leading angel and a very beautiful and talented one, at that. How can you get them to worship you instead of God?

You would have to be very careful about what you say, how you say it, and be cunning about your purpose.

Lucifer's purpose was to gain worship for himself. He could not openly accuse God because the angels would know he was lying, so he needed to plan his strategy and then carefully put it into action. Plan and strategize is precisely what Satan did.

One writer describes the start of the war in heaven like this:

> Leaving his place in the immediate presence of the Father, Lucifer went forth to diffuse the spirit of discontent among the angels. He worked with mysterious secrecy and for a time, concealed his real purpose under an appearance of reverence for God. He began to insinuate doubts concerning the laws that governed heavenly beings, intimating that though laws might be necessary for the inhabitants of the worlds, angels, being more exalted, needed no such restraint, for their own wisdom was a sufficient guide. They were not beings that could bring dishonour to God; all their thoughts were holy; it

was no more possible for them than for God Himself to err.[27]

By insinuating that they didn't need rules and that God was in some way inhibiting the angels and not allowing them the glory they should have, Satan made it seem like something was missing that he could fix if given the proper position. Satan began to bring disharmony to heaven and feelings of discontent in what had been a perfectly happy and loving environment.[28]

> While secretly fomenting discord and rebellion, he [Lucifer] with consummate craft caused it to appear as his sole purpose to promote loyalty and to preserve harmony and peace.[29]

Imagine what it must have been like when the whispers of Lucifer's discontent began circulating amongst the angels, who had only felt joy and peace before this.

> While there was no open outbreak division of feeling imperceptibly grew up among the angels. There were some who looked with favour upon Lucifer's insinuations against the government of God. …These stood ready to second Lucifer's demand for equal authority with the Son of God. … Christ was the Son of God; He had been one with Him before the angels were called into existence. He had ever stood at the right hand of the Father… The loyal angels could see only terrible consequences from this dissension, and with earnest entreaty they counselled the disaffected ones to renounce their purpose and prove themselves loyal to God by fidelity to His government.[30]

Now, where there had been harmony and joy, there was a conflict of loyalties. On the one hand, some reasoned that Lucifer wanted to improve things in heaven and on the other

---

[27] White, Ellen (1890) *Patriarchs and Prophets*, Review and Herald Publishing Association page 37.1
[28] Ibid.
[29] ibid, page 38.2
[30] Ibid. p.38.2,3

hand, there were those who saw that his stance was causing feelings of discontent that was not previously there.

Imagine now that you are Jesus, the Son of God, the leader of the angelic host. What would you do in the light of this conflict?

> The Son of God presented before [Lucifer] the greatness, the goodness, and the justice of the Creator, and the sacred, unchanging nature of His law. God Himself had established the order of heaven; and in departing from it, Lucifer would dishonour his Maker and bring ruin upon himself. But the warning, given in infinite love and mercy, only aroused a spirit of resistance. **Lucifer allowed his jealousy of Christ to prevail, and became the more determined.**[31]

Wow!

What would God do?

How can He answer the accusations made against Him?

What can God do to deal with Satan's lies and restore harmony in heaven?

> The law of love being the foundation of the government of God, the happiness of all intelligent beings depends upon their perfect accord with its great principles of righteousness. God desires from all His creatures the service of love—service that springs from an appreciation of His character. He takes no pleasure in a forced obedience; and to all He grants freedom of will, that they may render Him voluntary service.[32]

God could have destroyed Satan as soon as he became rebellious. If God had done that, it would have awakened an atmosphere of fear and given rise to more rebellion. Instead, God allowed Satan to continue in his rebellion. Over time Satan would reveal his character. The truth would be clearly seen.

---

[31] Ibid. p.35.3
[32] Ibid., p 34.3

Satan used this same method of insinuation and deception when he tempted Eve in the Garden of Eden. It is a tactic he still uses today. He misrepresents God's character so that people reject God or swear allegiance to God because of fear of punishment, but God is LOVE!

And so, through Millenia, Satan worked to lead humans into sin, away from love and service to God.

The Old Testament records how Satan moved to try to prevent the coming of the Messiah, and God's moves to ensure that the avenue for the Messiah was kept open.

If Satan could win all humanity to himself, there would be no one through whom God could work. As God does not force anyone, He would need someone willing to carry the Christ-child, ready to serve God, and willing to go through the pain of being the virgin mother.

In the Bible, the Book of Job records that Satan destroyed Job's family, took away all Job's possessions and even subjected Job to pain and disease in his attempt to get Job to abandon his faith in God. If Satan could get Job to renounce his faith in God, there would be no one left through whom God could make true His promise to save humanity through a descendent of Adam. Thus, he would effectively close down the avenue of the Saviour God promised Adam in **Genesis 3:15 (NIV).**

> [15] *And I will put enmity*
>   *between you and the woman,*
>   *and between your offspring[a] and hers;*
> *he will crush[b] your head,*
>   *and you will strike his heel."*

Footnotes

a. Genesis 3:15 Or *seed*
b. Genesis 3:15 Or *strike*

Satan had said that man couldn't keep the law of God, and throughout history, it may have appeared so. Even the faithful fell to sin, but God put enmity in human hearts so that there is an active battle against evil in the heart of those who wish to follow God.

Even the worst criminals have an internalised sense of right and wrong. This is the enmity that God placed inside us to help us recognise even as small children that something is wrong.

The offspring of Adam and Eve will suffer because of Satan's attack. This is how he strikes the heel of humans. However, in this text God is promising that a descendant of Adam and Eve will crush the serpent's head. The crushing of the head, Satan understood, was predicting his own destruction.

When Jesus is born, Satan sets things in motion to try to destroy the infant Jesus.

The Gospels record Satan's attempt to kill the Saviour following his birth. In his attempt, through Herod, all baby boys two years old and under in Bethlehem, and its districts were killed. Satan attempted to cause Jesus to sin, and therefore become disqualified to provide salvation to humanity.

Christ as a man would show that **it is possible** to live a life of selflessness, love, and fellowship with God, a sinless life.

St Matthew's gospel records the temptation of Jesus after His baptism.

In **Matthew 4:9,10**, Satan, speaking to Jesus says,

> [9] *"All this I will give you," he said, "if you will bow down and worship me."*
> [10] *Jesus said to him, "Away from me, Satan! It is written: 'Worship the Lord your God, and serve him only."*

The crux of the matter is Satan wants to be worshipped. He has been working throughout the ages to direct worship away from God. He does not care if you worship him directly or indirectly. His aim is you DO NOT WORSHIP GOD, THE CREATOR OF THE UNIVERSE, THE LIFE-GIVER!

> **But [Satan] was defeated. He could not lead Jesus into sin. He could not discourage Him, or drive Him from a work He had come on earth to do.** From the desert to Calvary, the storm of Satan's wrath beat upon [Jesus], but the more mercilessly it fell, the more firmly did the Son of God cling to the hand of His Father, ... All the efforts of Satan to oppress and overcome Him only brought out in a purer light His spotless character.[33]

Jesus came to live amongst us and overcome sin as a man because of His great love for us that He did it for us!

This fact gets me every time; that God would become man to save us, it leaves me without adequate words of gratitude.

What manner of love is this, that God would lay down His life for man?

> To the angels and the unfallen worlds, the cry, "It is finished," had a deep significance. ...

> Not until the death of Christ was the character of Satan clearly revealed to the angels or to the unfallen worlds. The arch-apostate had so clothed himself with deception that even holy beings had not understood his principles. They had not seen the nature of his rebellion.[34]

Now all was clear. The angels saw the love of God in action at the cross. The angels saw that even Satan had the freedom to choose what he wanted to do, good or evil. They saw that Satan and those who follow him chose evil.

Satan uses whatever methods he can. He continues to put humanity through trials, hardship and suffering to turn them from worshipping their Creator, but **Satan is a defeated foe**.

Even in our lives, this is the worst kind of warfare, where an accusation is made against you, and there is nothing you can do

---

[33] White, Ellen (1898) *Desire of the Ages*, Pacific Press Publishing Association , 759.4
[34] Ibid., p.758.2,3

to defend yourself or prove your innocence. Satan's accusations could only be answered as God allowed him the freedom to do as he wanted. In doing so, he showed his true self to the angels and the unfallen worlds.

For a short time, Satan thought he had won, but on resurrection morning, he realised God was the victor over sin and death.

- As a human, Jesus had lived a sinless life.
- As a human, Jesus had overcome the devil's temptations.
- As a human, Jesus had endured the suffering and shame that the devil put Him through.
- As a human, Jesus won the victory.

The Bible says, in **Isaiah 53:3-12 (NIV)**

> ³ *He was despised and rejected by mankind,*
> *a man of suffering, and familiar with pain.*
> *Like one from whom people hide their faces*
> *he was despised, and we held him in low esteem.*
> ⁴ *Surely he took up our pain*
> *and bore our suffering,*
> *yet we considered him punished by God,*
> *stricken by him, and afflicted.*
> ⁵ *But he was pierced for our transgressions,*
> *he was crushed for our iniquities;*
> *the punishment that brought us peace was on him,*
> *and by his wounds we are healed.*
> ⁶ *We all, like sheep, have gone astray,*
> *Each of us has turned to our own way;*
> *and the LORD has laid on him*
> *the iniquity of us all.*
> ⁷ *He was oppressed and afflicted,*
> *yet he did not open his mouth;*
> *he was led like a lamb to the slaughter,*
> *and as a sheep before its shearers is silent,*
> *so he did not open his mouth.*
> ⁸ *By oppression[a] and judgment he was taken away.*
> *Yet who of his generation protested?*

For he was cut off from the land of the living;
    for the transgression of my people he was punished.[b]
⁹ *He was assigned a grave with the wicked,*
    and with the rich in his death,
though he had done no violence,
    nor was any deceit in his mouth.
¹⁰ *Yet it was the LORD's will to crush him and cause him to suffer,*
    And though the LORD makes[c] *his life an offering for sin,*
He will see his offspring and prolong his days,
    And the will of the LORD will prosper in his hand.
¹¹ *After he has suffered,*
    He will see the light of life[d] *and be satisfied*[e]*;*
By his knowledge[f] *my righteous servant will justify many,*
    And he will bear their iniquities.
¹² *Therefore, I will give him a portion among the great,*[g]
    And he will divide the spoils with the strong,[h]
because he poured out his life unto death,
    and was numbered with the transgressors.
For he bore the sin of many,
    and made intercession for the transgressors.

Footnotes

a. Isaiah 53:8 Or *From arrest*
b. Isaiah 53:8 Or *generation considered / that he was cut off from the land of the living, / that he was punished for the transgression of my people?*
c. Isaiah 53:10 Hebrew *though you make*
d. Isaiah 53:11 Dead Sea Scrolls (see also Septuagint); Masoretic Text does not have *the light of life.*
e. Isaiah 53:11 Or (with Masoretic Text) ¹¹ *He will see the fruit of his suffering / and will be satisfied*
f. Isaiah 53:11 Or *by knowledge of him*
g. Isaiah 53:12 Or *many*
h. Isaiah 53:12 Or *numerous*

As a human, Jesus died to put right what was lost by Adam. The sovereignty of humanity was restored in the victory of Jesus.

I can imagine the joy in heaven when Jesus arrives after His mission on earth. I can hear them in joyful strains call out as in **Psalm 24:7-10**

> *Lift up your heads, O you gates!*
> *And be lifted up, you everlasting doors!*
> *And the King of glory shall come in.*
> *8 Who is this King of glory?*
> *The LORD strong and mighty,*
> *The LORD mighty in battle.*
> *9 Lift up your heads, O you gates!*
> *Lift up, you everlasting doors!*
> *And the King of glory shall come in.*
> *10 Who is this King of glory?*
> *The LORD of hosts,*
> *He is the King of glory. Selah*

Song:

Love was when God became a man
By Cortese Sisters (1975)[35]

Love was when God became a man,
locked in time and space, without rank or place.
Love was God born of Jewish kin;
Just a carpenter with some fishermen.
Love was when Jesus walked in history.
Lovingly He brought a new life that's free.
Love was God nailed to bleed and die,
to reach and love one such as I.

Love was when God became a man,
down where I could see. Love that reached to me.
Love was God dying for my sin;
And so trapped was I, my whole world caved in.
Love was when Jesus met me now it's real.
Lovingly He came; I can feel He's real.
Love was God; only He would try to reach,
to love one such as I

---

[35] Listen to or purchase Vinyl copies at:
https://www.discogs.com/release/11449322-Cortese-Sisters-Love-Was-When

Prayer

Dear God

Thank you for your love towards us, that you still came to earth and died for us even when we did not love you. You showed in your sacrifice that all men are worthy of your love. May we learn to love others, as you showed love to us. May we spread the good news of your love to others in Jesus' name.

Amen

Revelation 5: Mission Control (part five)

John records in **Revelation 5:6,7**

> *⁶ Then I saw a Lamb, looking as if it had been slain, standing at the center of the throne, encircled by the four living creatures and the elders. The Lamb had seven horns and seven eyes, which are the seven spirits of God sent out into all the earth. ⁷ He went and took the scroll from the right hand of him who sat on the throne.*

Jesus is the Lamb of God that was slain, and He is on the throne. He is surrounded by the four living creatures and the elders.

The Greek word used for lamb **ἀρνίον arníon**, pronounced **ar-nee'-on**; means: a lambkin or lamb. It describes a baby sheep less than a year old.

In this scene, the lamb on the throne also bears the marks of having been slain.

= Seven Spirits of God

---

³⁶ Pixels Allen, Paul (5ᵗʰ April 2021) The Lamb with Seven Horns and Seven Eyes, Internet cited on 05.02.2022 at: https://pixels.com/featured/the-lamb-with-seven-horns-and-seven-eyes-paul-allen.html

Now lambs are cute, but this lamb is different; it has horns. Sheep, when they are mature, have horns, but lambs do not have horns.

In nature, this lamb represents Christ as gentle as a lamb, but He was a mature man and matured in character when He died for us on the cross as a human.

On the lamb's head are seven horns. The seven horns represent perfect strength or power, and the seven eyes represent perfect vision. These we are told are the Sevenfold Spirit of God.

Hang on a minute; we have heard this term before. The church represented by the lampstand, all ablaze before the throne of God in **Revelation 4:5**, was said to be the Sevenfold Spirits of God.

So, what is this new imagery?

Jesus, the gentle lamb, in His full power and strength, with His perfect vision, carries the church, you and I, in His person, in Himself.

In Revelation Chapter 1, He is represented as carrying the seven messengers of the churches (the seven stars) in His hands. As the slain Lamb of God, He carries our humanity in His body, but at the same time, He is one with the Father and one with the Holy Spirit.

Humanity is adopted into divinity!

One of Satan's accusations is that God is arbitrary, self-centred, and must punish sin because that is His nature.

However, at the cross, all of the universe saw clearly, that God is LOVE! His love has no limits! He was prepared to die so that we could be saved!

Like the lambs in ancient Israel symbolically took on the sins of those who sacrificed them, Christ was willing to take on our sins on Himself.

Satan reminded all of the heavenly host that sin's wage is death. Humanity was guilty of sin. Therefore, death was their deserved lot.

The Bible tells us in **Romans 3:23 (NIV)**

> [23] *for all have sinned and fall short of the glory of God,*

Christ was willing to give up His position in heaven to pay that penalty for us. He was willing to die in our place.

What measure of love is this?

Pauls says, in **Romans 8:38,39**

> [38] *For I am convinced that neither death nor life, neither angels nor demons, neither the present nor the future, nor any powers,* [39] *neither height nor depth, nor anything else in all creation, will be able to separate us from the love of God that is in Christ Jesus our Lord.*

Sin carries a heavy penalty – DEATH!

Because Christ had not sinned, death had no hold on Him!

Christ had lived the perfect, sinless life. He took on himself our sins, and He offers us His righteousness.

Satan is a defeated foe.

- Jesus! – The Lion of the Tribe of Judah
- Jesus! – Michael, the commander of the heavenly host
- Jesus! – The archangel – leader of the angelic host
- Jesus! – The Prince of heaven, Daniel's Prince
- Jesus! – The Lamb of God

Has **defeated** Satan, our enemy, and **Jesus** is worthy to open the scroll in God's hand.

He defeated our enemy and offers us life eternal. Easter is the celebration of that victory!

Revelation 5:8 (NIV)

> [8] And when he had taken it, the four living creatures and the twenty-four elders fell down before the Lamb. Each one had a harp and they were holding golden bowls full of incense, which are the prayers of God's people.

When Christ accepted the scroll from God's right hand, he was symbolically accepting the role as the rightful sovereign of the earth forever, and humanity had now become part of the Kingdom of God.

Christ had redeemed us with His blood, and everyone on all the earth belongs to Him.

Let's see what Jesus told His disciples before he left the earth.

Acts 1:4,5 (NIV)

> [4] On one occasion, while he was eating with them, he gave them this command: "Do not leave Jerusalem, but wait for the gift my Father promised, which you have heard me speak about. [5] For John baptized with water, but in a few days, you will be baptized with the Holy Spirit."

John 14:26

> [26] But the Advocate, the Holy Spirit, whom the Father will send in my name, will teach you all things and will remind you of everything I have said to you.

So, what happened?

Acts 2:1-4

> **2** *When the day of Pentecost came, they were all together in one place.* **²** *Suddenly a sound like the blowing of a violent wind came from heaven and filled the whole house where they were sitting.* **³** *They saw what seemed to be tongues of fire that separated and came to rest on each of them.* **⁴** *All of them were filled with the Holy Spirit and began to speak in other tongues as the Spirit enabled them.*

Acts 2:1-40 (See Appendix 2) tells us that people from around the world gathered after they heard the sound, and Peter preached to them. Everyone heard in their own language, and some 3,000 people joined the new Christian Church that day. In this way, God allowed the message of his love and redemption to spread worldwide.

So why is this significant?

After the king's inauguration in Israel, the king's enemies would be dealt with or banished; then, gifts would be given to the king's loyal supporters. We have an example in the inauguration of King David in **2 Samuel chapters 8, 9** (See Appendix 3). David spends some time dealing with Israel's enemies. After that David gives to Mephibosheth all the lands that were King Saul's. He provides for him daily at his own table with his family after dealing with his enemies.

So, at Jesus' inauguration in heaven, just ten days after Jesus' ascension, on the Day of Pentecost, in that upper room in Jerusalem, Christ's promised gift, the Holy Spirit, was sent to the believers.

The Holy Spirit is Jesus' inauguration gift to humanity. The fullness of the Holy Spirit is sent to the earth to support, teach, and help us. The Holy Spirit speaks on the Creator's behalf to us.

We can sit at God's spiritual table every day as we allow the Holy Spirit to guide and teach us.

Revelation 5:8 (NIV)

> . [8] And when he had taken it, the four living creatures and the twenty-four elders fell down before the Lamb. Each one had a harp and they were holding golden bowls full of incense, which are the prayers of God's people.

The four living creatures and the twenty-four elders play a part in our salvation. These elders are holding a harp and a golden bowl of incense, which the text tells us are the prayers of God's people. As they offer the prayers of God's people, God responds. He gives directions in response to our prayers, which his angels carry out. We learnt this as we studied Revelation 4.

The four living creatures and the elders are overwhelmed by God's goodness and mercy towards us, and they fall before Jesus.

Note this:

When you cry out to God with a broken and contrite heart, God responds and sends His angels to help you. His mercy covers you, and He begins the work of change in you.

As you get to know God, you seek a change of heart, a change of disposition, a change of direction. You become aware of your failings and want to overcome your faults. Soon you realise that you can't change on your own, and you cry out to God as the Psalmist did.

Psalm 51:10 King James Version (KJV)

> [10] Create in me a clean heart, O God; and renew a right spirit within me.

Lord, change my heart.

Help me change the way I think.

Help me change my reactions.

Sometimes we are so overwhelmed by our weaknesses and failing that all we can say is, **"Lord help!"** Sometimes we can't even verbalise what we want in words or thoughts, and our spirit groans and our tears stream. The Holy Spirit understands your groans, and help is immediately sent to you.

Romans 8:26.27 says,

> [26] *In the same way, the Spirit helps us in our weakness. We do not know what we ought to pray for, but the Spirit himself intercedes for us through wordless groans.* [27] *And he who searches our hearts knows the mind of the Spirit, because the Spirit intercedes for God's people in accordance with the will of God.*

God knows exactly what you need to prepare you for life in His Kingdom. His mercy forgives you, and His judgement begins the work of cleaning you up because you cannot enter a holy kingdom full of sin.

That's why we can sing with Tremaine Hawkins,

> You changed my life complete
> And now I sit, I sit at my Saviour's feet.
> I'm not what I used to be,
> I'm not the same
> A wonderful change has come over me.
>
> You've changed my way of walking Lord
> You've changed the way of my talking Lord
> A wonderful change has come over me.

Do you know why the prayers of the saints are represented as incense?

When you and I pray, we acknowledge God as our Creator, Sustainer, Provider, Protector, Father, and Friend.

Prayer is sweet to God because prayer is victory.

Even in its weakest form, a prayer says, "I am looking to you, God; I acknowledge that you exist and you care for me!"

Your prayer may be: "God are you there? Can you hear me?"

Oh, God can hear you, and He is there! He is waiting for you to open your heart and mind to Him. Prayer is the beginning and the means to a rich relationship with God. Prayer gives us access to an all-powerful, loving, caring God who is pleased to give good gifts to his children. So, prayer is sweet incense to God!

Through Jesus' victory on the cross, the salvation of every believer was secure. Salvation is yours; all you have to do is accept it.

The twenty-four elders and the four creatures break out in song in their joy and complete adoration.

Revelation 5:9 (KJV)

> *9 And they sung a new song, saying, Thou art worthy to take the book, and to open the seals thereof: for thou wast slain, and hast redeemed us to God by thy blood out of every kindred, and tongue, and people, and nation;*

In the King James Version of the Bible, the twenty-four elders identify themselves as redeemed by the blood of the Lamb, which would make them human beings who have been translated to heaven. Perhaps they are those who were raised when Jesus resurrected mentioned in *Matthew 27:53-53*

> *52 and the tombs broke open. The bodies of many holy people who had died were raised to life. 53 They came out of the tombs after Jesus' resurrection and went into the holy city and appeared to many people.*

Modern translations from the original text do not identify the twenty-four elders in this way.

Revelation 5:9 (NIV)

> [9] *And they sang a new song, saying:*
> *"You are worthy to take the scroll*
> *and to open its seals,*
> *because you were slain,*
> *and with your blood you purchased for God*
> *persons from every tribe and language and people and*
> *nation.*

What does it mean 'with your blood you purchased for God persons from every tribe, language, people and nation?'

In some cultures, a bride is purchased from her family to enter another family. She would have no right to return to her family and would be subject to the functioning of the new family as a wife.

In our world's history, people were purchased as slaves. They had no freedom and worked for no reward until they died or were freed. They became the owner's possession and are subject to their owner's will. Sadly slavery still continues in our modern world.

Rarely, however, someone would be bought to be set free.

Matthew 20:28 (NIV) says,

> [28] *... the Son of Man did not come to be served, but to serve, and to give his life as a ransom for many."*

Ransom (noun) = a sum of money demanded or paid for the release of a captive.

Ransom (verb) = obtain the release of (a captive) by paying a ransom.

Definition from Oxford Languages Dictionary

The word translated as ransom is from the Greek term **Padah** pronounced **pä·dä'** means - to sever, i.e. ransom; generally, to release; preserve: deliver, redeem, or rescue.

Did Satan demand Christ's death as a payment from God for us?

NO! God cannot be manipulated.

Hosea 13:14 (NIV) sheds some light on what Jesus' death did,

> *¹⁴ "I will deliver this people from the power of the grave;*
> *I will redeem them from death.*
> *Where, O death, are your plagues?*
> *Where, O grave, is your destruction?*

So, Christ's death was to deliver us from the grave and redeem us from death.

What about a slave price? Are we bought to become slaves to God, persons with no freedom of choice?

No! We are not bought to become slaves to God, individuals with no freedom of choice.

So, what are we purchased for?

We are purchased to be set free!

We are delivered from sin and set free!

How are we purchased?

We cannot fully understand the great sacrifice Christ made for us to become human, endure a life of temptation and abuse, and then die publicly in a shameful.

Why did He do it?

Because His great love could not let us go, He would do His utmost to save whoever wants to be saved.

At the cross, Christ could have stopped Satan in his tracks and prevented Satan from killing his creator. He could have called the angels to His aid to vanquish Satan, but even on the cross, the Creator would allow Satan the freedom he was given from the time he was made. The freedom to make his own choices. Freedom is what Satan had argued that the angels didn't have. At the cross, they saw Satan was allowed uttermost freedom, but his purposes were not high and holy; they were evil. He so hated the Son of God that he would kill Him. Even in this, God allowed Satan his freedom.

Satan would have won if God had prevented him from following his free will. God's love would not compromise even in this. So, Christ gave up his life!

As we contemplate the love of God exhibited on Calvary and accept this as God's true character, we are freed from the chains of the enemy. We see that Satan seeks only to destroy us. We choose freely to follow Jesus. We must choose freely to give our life to Him, and Christ will help us break the chains of sin in our lives.

The Bible says in *John 8:36 (NIV)*

   36 So if the Son sets you free, you will be free indeed.

Free to believe in the forgiveness of God, as we realise that Jesus, the Son of God, forgave those who were mocking Him, beating Him, spitting on Him, whilst they were engaged in denouncing Him and orchestrating his death!

Free to believe in the love of God, as we realise the depths to which Christ stooped to save us. To become human forever! To die on a rugged cross so that freedom could still be maintained in His Kingdom.

That freedom brings with it JOY! We are overjoyed when we realise that **all that Christ accomplished in His sinless life, He offers us with no charge**.

No penance is needed!

No bill to pay!

Freedom is ours if we accept it!

Through Jesus, all who believe can be cleansed from sin and selfishness, and have their spirit renewed, so that they, with the help of the Holy Spirit, can keep the law of God, the law of love.

In other words, Jesus fixed the human problem of sin and made a way out of the cycle to eternal death. He has provided the Holy Spirit to help us keep the commandments of God.

With the Holy Spirit's help, we can

> Love the Lord our God with all our heart, and with all our soul, and with all our mind, as well as love our neighbour as ourselves. **(Matthew 22:37-39)**

Jesus accomplished for us what we could not accomplish for ourselves.

Amen! Amen! Amen!

The angels watched the life of Christ as a human. His life showed that a man could live a holy, sinless life. They watched as Christ allowed the devil and his angels to do what they wanted to do. Satan wanted the Son of God dead. So, before the onlooking universe, he carried out his plan, and Jesus died, as was prophesied.

On the third day, despite the Roman soldiers' guard, despite the host of evil angels that held the watch,[38] Gabriel arrives, calling the Son of God, and in a flash, Christ the Son of God, one with the Father and one with man arose from the grave.

Satan had done all he could to prevent the Saviour from living a sinless life. He had done all he could to keep Christ in the grave. Death had no claim on Jesus. The grave could not hold Him who had created the land and sea. He who is the source of life could not be held in death.

Satan lost the battle!

---

[38] White, E. G, (1898) *The Desire of Ages,* Pacific Press Publishing Association, p.779.1

The angels now fully understood what Satan's purpose was. He could no longer come to them with his cunning lies. He had exposed who he was, and they would have no more of him. Heaven was now out of bounds for him because no one would listen to him. He was defeated.

Revelation 5:10

> ^{10} You have made them to be a kingdom and priests to serve our God, and they will reign on the earth."

We who have been redeemed by the blood of the Lamb are priests on this earth. With the help of the Holy Spirit, it is through us that this gospel of God's Kingdom of love is to be preached in the world. To people from every nation, kingdom and family, salvation is offered.

Revelation 5:11

> ^{11} Then I looked and heard the voice of many angels, numbering thousands upon thousands, and ten thousand times ten thousand. They encircled the throne and the living creatures and the elders.

John sees many angels encircle the throne of God and the elders and the creatures. He describes this as ten thousand times ten thousand. 10,000 x 10,000 = 100,000,000. One hundred million is not an exact number; it was John's way of saying more than you can imagine; a large number of angels.

Revelation 5:12-14

> ^{12} In a loud voice they were saying:
> "Worthy is the Lamb, who was slain,
> to receive power and wealth and wisdom and strength
> and honour and glory and praise!"
> ^{13} Then I heard every creature in heaven and on earth
> and under the earth and on the sea, and all that is in
> them, saying:
> "To him who sits on the throne and to the Lamb
> be praise and honour and glory and power,

for ever and ever!"
¹⁴The four living creatures said, "Amen," and the elders
fell down and worshiped.

Over the millennia of Earth's history, a battle has been going on.
Jesus has won the battle. He is still gathering His people. The
battle is not a physical battle. Guns, swords and bombs are not
employed in this war. It is a war over the rightful sovereignty and
authority of God. It is a war of ideas. It's a war about who is
worthy of our worship and praise.

Is God a loving, caring ruler, worthy of our worship and praise, or
is He arbitrary and exacting, an angry God waiting to destroy
those who don't follow Him? Does He offer us freedom or
slavery?

Just as He allowed the angels freedom to decide, God leaves
you free to decide who you will worship.

Songs:

The love of God 1917
Frederick M. Lehman, (7 Aug 1868 - 20 Feb 1953)
v. 3 by Anonymous/Unknown

1. The love of God is greater far
   Than tongue or pen can ever tell;
   It goes beyond the highest star,
   And reaches to the lowest hell;
   The guilty pair, bowed down with care,
   God gave His Son to win;
   His erring child He reconciled,
   And pardoned from his sin.

   Refrain:
   Oh, love of God, how rich and pure!
   How measureless and strong!
   It shall forevermore endure—
   The saints' and angels' song.

2. When hoary time shall pass away,
   And earthly thrones and kingdoms fall,
   When men who here refuse to pray,
   On rocks and hills and mountains call,
   God's love so sure, shall still endure,
   All measureless and strong;
   Redeeming grace to Adam's race—
   The saints' and angels' song.

3. Could we with ink the ocean fill,
   And were the skies of parchment made,
   Were every stalk on earth a quill,
   And every man a scribe by trade;
   To write the love of God above
   Would drain the ocean dry;
   Nor could the scroll contain the whole,
   Though stretched from sky to sky.

Prayer

Dear God

You are most worthy of our praise and our worship.
You deserve all the glory and honour of every being in the universe.

You have paid the penalty for our sin and given us freedom.
Help us to use our freedom to your honour and glory every day, in Jesus' name.

Amen.

Key Words and Phrases

Accuser of the brethren – Satan

Archangel – Jesus

Atonement cover/Mercy seat – place above the Ark and under the wings of the cherubim where the voice of God was heard.

Blazing lampstand – the church empowered by the Holy Spirit

Bowl full of incense – prayers of the saints

Clothed in white - righteous

Dragon – Satan

Flashes of lightning and peels of thunder – the voice of God

Him who sits on the throne – God the Father

Lamb that was slain – Jesus

Living creatures and Cherubim – symbols of the all seeing all responsive services to humanity by angels of God.

Lucifer /king of Tyre – Satan

Michael/Chief Prince/Daniel's Prince – Jesus

Open door – the start of the salvation process

Seven lampstands – the church

Sevenfold spirit – the Holy Spirit

Shekinah glory – the light that appeared above the Mercy Seat/Atonement cover indicating God's presence.

Son of Man – a title of Christ

Tent of meeting - the tabernacle

The Lion of the tribe of Judah – Jesus

The Root of David – Jesus, descendant of David

Twenty-four elders wearing crowns and seated on thrones – twenty-four rulers

About the author

As a Christian who put her trust in God from an early age, Linda has dedicated her life to sharing God's messages of love. She has attended the Seventh-Day Adventist Church since childhood.

Her home is in London where she lives with her husband of over 40 years and has been blessed with three adult daughters and two grandchildren.

Born in Trinidad, she arrived in the U.K. at the age of 11 and has enjoyed being an active part of her local church community ever since. As a person with a passion for serving others, Linda has run many Bible Study groups, Children's Ministries programmes, and Youth programmes. She is involved in community outreach and is also a qualified lay preacher and Church Elder. In her professional life, she is an award-winning advisor to young people supporting her clients through difficult times.

Linda holds a Bachelor's degree in Education and English Literature. Her love for God and enjoyment of literature has led Linda to study the Bible in-depth as she seeks to nurture and grow her faith and relationship with Jesus. This love of reading and learning has led Linda to become a book editor and now, an author too.

Email: lindagreenrevelations@gmail.com

LinkedIn: linkedin.com/in/linda-green-author

Instagram: @lindagreenauthor

References

Circe Institute, Phillips, Brian (30th May 2017) "A walk through the Tabernacle", Internet cited on 26.11.2021 at: https://www.pngkit.com/downpic/u2q8y3o0a9o0r5u2_layout-of-the-tabernacle-tabernacle-dimensions/

CRC, "The Sanctuary Service", Internet cited on 16.11.2021 at: https://www.crcbermuda.com/bible/the-sanctuary/the-sanctuary-service/chapter-11-the-daily-service

Eye of Prophecy, Garybowers, (27 June 2015) "The Ark of the Covenant...Part II", Internet cited on 18.11.2021 at: https://eyeofprophecy.com/2015/06/27/the-ark-of-the-covenant-part-ii/

Free Bible Images, "The ark of the covenant", Internet cited on 09.06.2022 at: https://www.freebibleimages.org/illustrations/bs-ark-covenant/

Maxwell C. Mervyn (1985) *God Cares, Vol 2: The Message of Revelation for you and your family,* Pacific Publishing Association, Ontario, Canada

Peckham, John C, (2018) *Theodicy of Love; Cosmic Conflict and the Problem of Evil,* Baker Academic, USA

Plant, Renee, (3rd July 2021) "Michael Name Meaning", Internet cited on 02.12.2021 at: https://www.verywellfamily.com/michael-name-meaning-5115812

Sefaria, "Mishnah Tamid", 3:2, Internet cited on 16.11.2021 at: https://www.sefaria.org/Mishnah_Tamid.1.1?lang=bi

The Bible Says, "Exodus 40:1-16", Internet cited on 17.11.2021 at: https://thebiblesays.com/commentary/exod/exod-40/exodus-401-16/

VoiceTube, "Ezekiel's Astonishing Vision of God", Internet cited on 17.11.2021 at: https://www.voicetube.com/videos/78522

Wikimedia Commons, Dororenko (18 June 2010) "File:2010 - red jasper.jpg", Internet cited on 16.11.2021 at: https://commons.wikimedia.org/wiki/File:2010_-_red_jasper.jpg

Wikimedia Commons, "File:1 lapis lazuli.jpg", Internet cited on 17.11.2021 at: https://commons.wikimedia.org/wiki/File:1_lapis_lazuli.jpg

Wikipedia Commons "File: Menorah 0307.jpg", Internet cited on 01.09.2021 at: https://commons.wikimedia.org/wiki/File:Menorah_0307.jpg

Wikimedia Commons, Geni (July 2018) "File: Duke of Devonshire Emerald.JPG", Internet cited on 16.11.2021 at: https://commons.wikimedia.org/wiki/File:Duke_of_Devonshire_Emerald.JPG

Wikimedia Commons, Lavinsky, Robert M, (March 2010) "File:Corundum-215330.jpg", Internet cited on 16.11.2021 at: https://commons.wikimedia.org/wiki/File:Corundum-215330.jpg

Wikipedia, "Sanctuary Lamp", Internet cited on 16.11.2021 at: https://en.wikipedia.org/wiki/Sanctuary_lamp

White, Ellen (1898) *Desire of the Ages*, Pacific Press Publishing Association

White, Ellen (1890) *Patriarchs and Prophets*, Review and Herald Publishing Association

White, Ellen (13 December 1892) *The Review and Herrald,* par 7, Internet on cited 16.11.21 at: https://m.egwwritings.org/en/book/821.12368

YAHUSHUA HA MASHIACH) THE CHIEF CORNERSTONE Ministry Congregation, Glasgow (Scotland, U.K.) "The

"MISHKAN/Tabernacle of Moshe/Moses", Internet cited on 28.12.21 at: https://yahushua-thechiefcornerstone.com/the-tabernacle-of-moshe-moses/

Appendix 1 - Angel interventions in the Bible

Throughout the Bible, we have evidence of the work the angels of God do in our world.

- In Genesis 3:24 at the garden of Eden following the fall of man, Cherubim are said to guard the way to the tree of life.
- In Exodus 26:1,31 Cherubim are embroidered into the veils/curtains of the tabernacle and in 1 Kings 6, cherubim cover the ceilings, walls and doors of the sanctuary coverings representing the work they carry out between heaven and earth.
- In Numbers 7:89 we are told that Moses heard the voice of God speaking to him from off the mercy seat that was upon the ark … from between the two cherubim.
- In 2 Kings 19:15, Hezekiah, king of Israel, said as he prayed, "O Lord God of Israel, enthroned between the cherubim, you alone are God over all the kingdoms of the earth. You have made heaven and earth.
- In Genesis 16, the angel of the Lord attends to Hagar after Hagar ran away from Sarah.
- In Genesis 19, two angels rescue Lot and his family before Sodom is destroyed.
- In Genesis 21:17,18, the angel of God spoke to Hagar when she and her son were sent away from Abraham and showed her a well, telling Hagar how God would bless Ishmael.
- In Genesis 22:11, the angel of the Lord stopped Abraham from sacrificing Isaac.
- In Genesis 28:12, Jacob dreams of a ladder/stairway between heaven and earth, and the angels of God were ascending and descending on it.
- In Genesis 32:1, The angels of God met Jacob on his way to meet Esau.

- In Exodus 3:2 The angel of the Lord appears to Moses in the burning bush
- In Exodus 23, The angel is said to go before the children of Israel as they journey in the wilderness.
- In Numbers 22, Balaam is stopped by the angel of the Lord as he travels to Balak.
- In Judges 2, The angel of the Lord speaks to the people of Israel at Bokim.
- In Judges 6, The angel of the Lord appears to Gideon at the oak of Ophrah
- In Judges 13, The angel of the Lord appears to Manoah's barren wife and tells her she will have a son, giving her health instructions to follow throughout her pregnancy. He also speaks with Manoah about the birth.
- In 1 Kings 19, an angel wakes Elijah, who is depressed and running away from Jezebel, who threatened to kill him.
- In 2 Kings 1, The angel of the Lord guides Elijah regarding the king of Samaria.
- In 2 Kings 19, The angel of the Lord defeats the Assyrian army that came to conquer Israel.
- In the book of Job, The story tells us of angels' gatherings as they report to God, but it also tells of the angel we know as Satan, who throws calamities on Job, the servant of God.
- In Daniel 6, God sent an angel to shut the lions' mouths so that Daniel's life is preserved, and King Cyrus could learn of the God of heaven and earth.
- In Zechariah 1-3, In Zechariah's vision, he is shown Satan accusing the people of God. Still, the angels give the high priest a clean turban and clean clothes representing the removal of our sin, which is replaced by clothing representing the righteousness of Christ.
- In Matthew 1; Luke 1, an angel appears to Mary to tell her that she will bear the Messiah. An angel tells Joseph of

the pregnancy and tells him the child is conceived of the Holy Spirit.

- In Matthew 2, an angel tells Joseph to take Jesus to Egypt to escape Herod's attempt to kill Jesus. An angel tells Joseph it is safe to return to Israel as Herod is now dead.
- In Matthew 4; Mark 1, angels attend to Jesus after the temptation by Satan.
- In Matthew 28, an angel of the Lord rolled the stone away from Jesus' tomb.
- In Luke 1, an angel of the Lord tells Zechariah that his wife Elizabeth will have a baby they were to call John.
- In Luke 2, angels appear to shepherds to tell them of Jesus' birth.
- In Luke 24:23, angels tell the women that Jesus is alive.
- In John 20:12, two angels sat in the tomb where Jesus had laid.
- In Acts 5, the apostles are released from jail by an angel of the Lord.
- In Acts 8, an angel of the Lord tells Philip to go from Jerusalem to Gaza, and as a result, Philip teaches an Ethiopian eunuch the gospel.
- In Acts 11, an angel appears to Cornelius and tells him to send for Peter.
- In Acts 12, Peter is released from prison by an angel.
- In Acts 27, an angel of the Lord tells Paul that the ship will be wrecked, but everyone on board will get to safety.

Appendix 2 – Acts 2:1-40

The Holy Spirit Comes at Pentecost

2 When the day of Pentecost came, they were all together in one place. [2] Suddenly a sound like the blowing of a violent wind came from heaven and filled the whole house where they were sitting. [3] They saw what seemed to be tongues of fire that separated and came to rest on each of them. [4] All of them were filled with the Holy Spirit and began to speak in other tongues[a] as the Spirit enabled them.
[5] Now there were staying in Jerusalem God-fearing Jews from every nation under heaven. [6] When they heard this sound, a crowd came together in bewilderment, because each one heard their own language being spoken. [7] Utterly amazed, they asked: "Aren't all these who are speaking Galileans? [8] Then how is it that each of us hears them in our native language? [9] Parthians, Medes and Elamites; residents of Mesopotamia, Judea and Cappadocia, Pontus and Asia,[b] [10] Phrygia and Pamphylia, Egypt and the parts of Libya near Cyrene; visitors from Rome [11] (both Jews and converts to Judaism); Cretans and Arabs—we hear them declaring the wonders of God in our own tongues!" [12] Amazed and perplexed, they asked one another, "What does this mean?"
[13] Some, however, made fun of them and said, "They have had too much wine."

Peter Addresses the Crowd

[14] Then Peter stood up with the Eleven, raised his voice and addressed the crowd: "Fellow Jews and all of you who live in Jerusalem, let me explain this to you; listen carefully to what I say. [15] These people are not drunk, as you suppose. It's only nine in the morning! [16] No, this is what was spoken by the prophet Joel:
[17] "'In the last days, God says,
    I will pour out my Spirit on all people.
Your sons and daughters will prophesy,
    your young men will see visions,

83

your old men will dream dreams.
[18] Even on my servants, both men and women,
    I will pour out my Spirit in those days,
    and they will prophesy.
[19] I will show wonders in the heavens above
    and signs on the earth below,
    blood and fire and billows of smoke.
[20] The sun will be turned to darkness
    and the moon to blood
    before the coming of the great and glorious day of the Lord.
[21] And everyone who calls
    on the name of the Lord will be saved.'[c]

[22] "Fellow Israelites, listen to this: Jesus of Nazareth was a man accredited by God to you by miracles, wonders and signs, which God did among you through him, as you yourselves know. [23] This man was handed over to you by God's deliberate plan and foreknowledge; and you, with the help of wicked men,[d] put him to death by nailing him to the cross. [24] But God raised him from the dead, freeing him from the agony of death, because it was impossible for death to keep its hold on him. [25] David said about him:

"'I saw the Lord always before me.
    Because he is at my right hand,
    I will not be shaken.
[26] Therefore my heart is glad and my tongue rejoices;
    my body also will rest in hope,
[27] because you will not abandon me to the realm of the dead,
    you will not let your holy one see decay.
[28] You have made known to me the paths of life;
    you will fill me with joy in your presence.'[e]

[29] "Fellow Israelites, I can tell you confidently that the patriarch David died and was buried, and his tomb is here to this day. [30] But he was a prophet and knew that God had promised him on oath that he would place one of his descendants on his throne. [31] Seeing what was to come, he spoke of the resurrection of the Messiah, that he was not abandoned to the realm of the dead, nor did his body see decay. [32] God has raised this Jesus to life, and we are all witnesses of it. [33] Exalted to the right hand of God, he has received from the Father the promised Holy

Spirit and has poured out what you now see and hear. **34** For David did not ascend to heaven, and yet he said,

"'The Lord said to my Lord:
  "Sit at my right hand
35 until I make your enemies
  a footstool for your feet."'[f]

36 "Therefore let all Israel be assured of this: God has made this Jesus, whom you crucified, both Lord and Messiah."

37 When the people heard this, they were cut to the heart and said to Peter and the other apostles, "Brothers, what shall we do?"

38 Peter replied, "Repent and be baptized, every one of you, in the name of Jesus Christ for the forgiveness of your sins. And you will receive the gift of the Holy Spirit. **39** The promise is for you and your children and for all who are far off—for all whom the Lord our God will call."

40 With many other words he warned them; and he pleaded with them, "Save yourselves from this corrupt generation." **41** Those who accepted his message were baptized, and about three thousand were added to their number that day.

Appendix 3 - 2 Samuel 8 and 9

David's Victories

8 In the course of time, David defeated the Philistines and subdued them, and he took Metheg Ammah from the control of the Philistines.

2 David also defeated the Moabites. He made them lie down on the ground and measured them off with a length of cord. Every two lengths of them were put to death, and the third length was allowed to live. So the Moabites became subject to David and brought him tribute.

3 Moreover, David defeated Hadadezer son of Rehob, king of Zobah, when he went to restore his monument at[a] the Euphrates River. **4** David captured a thousand of his chariots, seven thousand charioteers[b] and twenty thousand foot soldiers. He hamstrung all but a hundred of the chariot horses.

5 When the Arameans of Damascus came to help Hadadezer king of Zobah, David struck down twenty-two thousand of them. **6** He put garrisons in the Aramean kingdom of Damascus, and the Arameans became subject to him and brought tribute. The LORD gave David victory wherever he went.

7 David took the gold shields that belonged to the officers of Hadadezer and brought them to Jerusalem. **8** From Tebah[c] and Berothai, towns that belonged to Hadadezer, King David took a great quantity of bronze.

9 When Tou[d] king of Hamath heard that David had defeated the entire army of Hadadezer, **10** he sent his son Joram[e] to King David to greet him and congratulate him on his victory in battle over Hadadezer, who had been at war with Tou. Joram brought with him articles of silver, of gold and of bronze.

11 King David dedicated these articles to the LORD, as he had done with the silver and gold from all the nations he had subdued: **12** Edom[f] and Moab, the Ammonites and the Philistines, and Amalek. He also dedicated the plunder taken from Hadadezer son of Rehob, king of Zobah.

13 And David became famous after he returned from striking down eighteen thousand Edomites[g] in the Valley of Salt.

¹⁴ He put garrisons throughout Edom, and all the Edomites became subject to David. The LORD gave David victory wherever he went.

David's Officials

¹⁵ David reigned over all Israel, doing what was just and right for all his people. ¹⁶ Joab son of Zeruiah was over the army; Jehoshaphat son of Ahilud was recorder; ¹⁷ Zadok son of Ahitub and Ahimelek son of Abiathar were priests; Seraiah was secretary; ¹⁸ Benaiah son of Jehoiada was over the Kerethites and Pelethites; and David's sons were priests.

David and Mephibosheth

9 David asked, "Is there anyone still left of the house of Saul to whom I can show kindness for Jonathan's sake?"
² Now there was a servant of Saul's household named Ziba. They summoned him to appear before David, and the king said to him, "Are you Ziba?"
"At your service," he replied.
³ The king asked, "Is there no one still alive from the house of Saul to whom I can show God's kindness?"
Ziba answered the king, "There is still a son of Jonathan; he is lame in both feet."
⁴ "Where is he?" the king asked.
Ziba answered, "He is at the house of Makir son of Ammiel in Lo Debar."
⁵ So King David had him brought from Lo Debar, from the house of Makir son of Ammiel.
⁶ When Mephibosheth son of Jonathan, the son of Saul, came to David, he bowed down to pay him honor.
David said, "Mephibosheth!"
"At your service," he replied.
⁷ "Don't be afraid," David said to him, "for I will surely show you kindness for the sake of your father Jonathan. I will restore to you all the land that belonged to your grandfather Saul, and you will always eat at my table."
⁸ Mephibosheth bowed down and said, "What is your servant, that you should notice a dead dog like me?"

⁹ Then the king summoned Ziba, Saul's steward, and said to him, "I have given your master's grandson everything that belonged to Saul and his family. ¹⁰ You and your sons and your servants are to farm the land for him and bring in the crops, so that your master's grandson may be provided for. And Mephibosheth, grandson of your master, will always eat at my table." (Now Ziba had fifteen sons and twenty servants.)

¹¹ Then Ziba said to the king, "Your servant will do whatever my lord the king commands his servant to do." So Mephibosheth ate at David's[a] table like one of the king's sons.

¹² Mephibosheth had a young son named Mika, and all the members of Ziba's household were servants of Mephibosheth. ¹³ And Mephibosheth lived in Jerusalem, because he always ate at the king's table; he was lame in both feet.

Footnotes
2 Samuel 9:11 Septuagint; Hebrew *my*

Printed in Great Britain
by Amazon

30679397R00059